I0372443

श्रीअन्नपूर्णा पूजा च सहस्रनाम

Śrī Annapūrṇā Pūjā and Thousand Names

By

स्वामी सत्यानन्द सरस्वती

Swami Satyananda Saraswati

स्वामी विट्ठलानन्द सरस्वती

Swami Vittalananda Saraswati

माता पार्वतीनन्द सरस्वती

Mātā Parvatīnanda Saraswati

Published By

Devi Mandir Publications

Sunstar Publishers Ltd.

श्रीअन्नपूर्णा पूजा च सहस्रनाम

Śrī Annapūrṇā Pūjā and Thousand Names

by Devi Mandir Publications
5950 Highway 128
Napa, CA 94558 USA
Communications: Phone and Fax 1-707-966-2802
E-Mail swamiji@shreemaa.org
Please visit us on the World Wide Web at
http://www.shreemaa.org

ISBN 978-1-877795-08-4
Library of Congress Catalog Card Number
CIP 2001 126148

श्रीअन्नपूर्णा पूजा च सहस्रनाम
Śrī Annapūrṇā Pūjā and Thousand Names
Swami Satyananda Saraswati
1. Hindu Religion. 2. Worship. 3. Spirituality.
4. Philosophy. I. Saraswati, Swami Satyananda;
Saraswati, Swami Vittalananda;
Saraswati, Mātā Parvatīnanda Saraswati

Introduction

Anna means food and grains. Pūrṇā means full, complete and perfect. Annapūrṇā is the respected Supreme Goddess, She who is full, complete and perfect in food and grains. She is the symbol for the One who grants nourishment on every level.

She is called the Supreme Goddess of the City of Kāśī. Actually Ka means the cause; ā means the manifestation of consciousness; śa means peace and ī is the causal body. Kāśī is the place which causes consciousness to manifest the highest peace of the causal body. And She is the Supreme Goddess of the City of Kāśī.

Even Lord Śiva had to come to Her to beg alms. The famous verse which all sannyasis are required to learn proclaims:

अन्नपूर्णे सदा पूर्णे शङ्करप्राणवल्लभे ।
ज्ञानवैराग्यसिद्ध्यर्थं भिक्षां देहि च पार्वति ॥

annapūrṇe sadā pūrṇe śaṅkaraprāṇavallabhe |
jñānavairāgyasiddharytharh
bhikṣāṁ dehi ca pārvati ||

Oh Annapūrṇā, who is always full, complete and perfect, beloved energy of Lord Śiva, for the attainment of perfection in wisdom and renunciation give me alms, Pārvati.

That aspect of Pārvati who grants nourishment is called Annapūrṇā. She is the strength or force of life of Śiva, the beloved energy. He is incomplete without Her.

Why does Śiva want Her nourishment? For the attainment of perfection in wisdom and renunciation. That is Her gift to us all. Her wisdom teaches us that spirituality is about giving. The renunciation She teaches allows us to be in equanimity in every circumstance of life.

Mother Annapūrṇā inspires us to nourish others, to give our best, consistent in the wisdom that the greatest joy comes from renunciation. As we can free ourselves from attachment to our selfish considerations, we experience more and more of the bliss of Śaṅkara, the name of Śiva which literally means the cause of peace.

A thousand names of the Goddess Annapūrṇā are presented here, along with the famous Annapūrṇā Stotraṁ by Śaṅkarācārya. Also included are a hundred and eight names and Her meditations.

I remember Her kindness in allowing us to perform worship in Her famous Śakti Pīṭha temple in Varanasi. For nine days we performed Her pūjā, recited the Chaṇḍī Pāṭhaḥ and recited these thousand names before the sacred homa fire enkindled within the temple. What joy She bestows no one can describe, and I hope that the publication of this book will allow others to experience the wonder of Her nourishment.

Swami Satyananda Saraswati
Devi Mandir, 2001

देवता प्रणाम्
devatā praṇām

श्रीमन्महागणाधिपतये नमः
śrīmanmahāgaṇādhipataye namaḥ
We bow to the Respected Great Lord of Wisdom.

लक्ष्मीनारायणाभ्यां नमः
lakṣmīnārāyaṇābhyāṁ namaḥ
We bow to Lakṣmī and Nārāyaṇa, The Goal of all Existence and the Perceiver of All.

उमामहेश्वराभ्यां नमः
umāmaheśvarābhyāṁ namaḥ
We bow to Umā and Maheśvara, She who protects existence, and the Great Consciousness or Seer of All.

वाणीहिरण्यगर्भाभ्यां नमः
vāṇīhiraṇyagarbhābhyāṁ namaḥ
We bow to Vāṇī and Hiraṇyagarbha, Sarasvatī and Brahmā, who create the cosmic existence.

शचीपुरन्दराभ्यां नमः
śacīpurandarābhyāṁ namaḥ
We bow to Śacī and Purandara, Indra and his wife, who preside over all that is divine.

मातापितृभ्यां नमः
mātāpitṛbhyāṁ namaḥ
We bow to the Mothers and Fathers.

इष्टदेवताभ्यो नमः
iṣṭadevatābhyo namaḥ
We bow to the chosen deity of worship.

कुलदेवताभ्यो नमः
kuladevatābhyo namaḥ
We bow to the family deity of worship.

ग्रामदेवताभ्यो नमः
grāmadevatābhyo namaḥ
We bow to the village deity of worship.

वास्तुदेवताभ्यो नमः
vāstudevatābhyo namaḥ
We bow to the particular household deity of worship.

स्थानदेवताभ्यो नमः
sthānadevatābhyo namaḥ
We bow to the established deity of worship.

सर्वेभ्यो देवेभ्यो नमः
sarvebhyo devebhyo namaḥ
We bow to all the Gods.

सर्वेभ्यो ब्राह्मणेभ्यो नमः
sarvebhyo brāhmaṇebhyo namaḥ
We bow to all the Knowers of Divinity.

अन्नपूर्णा ध्यानम्
annapūrṇā dhyānam

- 1 -

अर्कोन्मुक्तशशाङ्ककोटिवदनामापीनितुङ्गस्तनीं
चन्द्रार्धाङ्कितमस्तकां मधुमदामालोलनेत्रत्रयीम् ।
बीभ्राणामनिशं वरं जपपटीं शूलं कपालं करै -
राद्यां योवनगर्वितां लिपितनूं वागीश्वरीमाश्रये ॥

arkonmuktaśaśāṅka
koṭivadanāmāpīnituṅgastanīṁ
candrārdhāṅkitamastakāṁ
madhumadāmālolanetratrayīm |
bībhrāṇāmaniśaṁ varaṁ
japapaṭīṁ śūlaṁ kapālaṁ karai-
rādyāṁ yovanagarvitāṁ
lipitanūṁ vāgīśvarīmāśrayai ||

The pearls of her necklace shine like millions of suns, the digit of the moon rests upon her head, and intoxicating sweetness exudes from the third eye of her forehead. She displays the mudrā granting boons, the japa mālā, the spear and skull in her hands. She is beautiful, anointed with the pride of youth. I take refuge in the Supreme Goddess of all vibrations.

- 2 -

रक्तं विचित्रवसनां नवचन्द्रचूडां
अन्न - प्रदाननिरतां स्तनभारनम्राम् ।
नृत्यन्तमिन्दु - सकलाभरणं विलोक्य
हृष्टां भजे भगवतीं भवदुःखहन्त्रीम् ॥

raktaṁ vicitravasanāṁ navacandracūḍāṁ
anna - pradānaniratāṁ stanabhāranamrām |
nṛtyantamindu - sakalābharaṇaṁ vilokya
hṛṣṭāṁ bhaje bhagavatīṁ bhavaduḥkhahantrīm ||

She wears a beautiful red colored cloth, and the new digit of the moon is shining in her hair. She is constantly engaged in giving food, her breasts are full, heavy with fullness, and she is watching the moon dancing upon the forehead of her beloved husband Śiva. She destroys the pain from all the individuals in the unlimited ocean of existence, she is extremely delighted. I serve the Goddess, the Mother of the Universe, Annapūrṇā.

ॐ अग्निर्ज्योतिर्ज्योतिरग्निः स्वाहा ।
सूर्यो ज्योतिर्ज्योतिः सूर्यः स्वाहा ।
अग्निर्वर्चो ज्योतिर्वर्चः स्वाहा ।
सूर्यो वर्चो ज्योतिर्वर्चः स्वाहा ।
ज्योतिः सूर्यः सूर्यो ज्योतिः स्वाहा ॥

oṁ agnir jyotir jyotir agniḥ svāhā
sūryo jyotir jyotiḥ sūryaḥ svāhā
agnir varco jyotir varcaḥ svāhā
sūryo varco jyotir varcaḥ svāhā
jyotiḥ sūryaḥ sūryo jyotiḥ svāhā

Oṁ The Divine Fire is the Light, and the Light is the Divine Fire; I am One with God! The Light of Wisdom is the Light, and the Light is the Light of Wisdom; I am One with God! The Divine Fire is the offering, and the Light is the Offering; I am One with God! The Light of Wisdom is the Offering, and the Light is the Light of Wisdom; I am One with God!

(Wave light)

ॐ अग्निर्ज्योती रविर्ज्योतिश्चन्द्रो ज्योतिस्तथैव च ।
ज्योतिषामुत्तमो देवी दीपोऽयं प्रतिगृह्यताम् ॥
ॐ ऐं ह्रीं श्रीं क्लीं नमो भगवति माहेश्वरिअन्नपूर्णे दीपं
समर्पयामि ॥

oṁ agnirjyotī ravirjyotiścandro jyotistathaiva ca
jyotiṣāmuttamo devī dīpo-yaṁ pratigṛhyatām
oṁ aiṁ hrīṁ śrīṁ klīṁ namo bhagavati māheśvari
annapūrṇe dīpaṁ samarpayāmi

Oṁ The Divine Fire is the Light, the Light of Wisdom is the Light, the Light of Devotion is the Light as well. The Light of the Highest Bliss, Oh Goddess, is in the Light that we offer, the Light that we request you to accept. The Infinite beyond Conception, Wisdom, Māyā, the perfection of peace in the mind and in the heart, the cause of union between the gross body and causal bodies of existence, I bow to the respected Supreme Goddess, She who is full, complete and perfect in food and grains with the offering of Light.

(Wave incense)

ॐ वनस्पतिरसोत्पन्नो गन्धात्ययी गन्ध उत्तमः ।
आघ्रेयः सर्वदेवानां धूपोऽयं प्रतिगृह्यताम् ॥
ॐ ऐं ह्रीं श्रीं क्लीं नमो भगवति माहेश्वरिअन्नपूर्णे धूपं
समर्पयामि ॥

oṁ vanaspatirasotpanno
gandhātyayī gandha uttamaḥ
āghreyaḥ sarvadevānāṁ dhūpo-yaṁ pratigṛhyatām
oṁ aiṁ hrīṁ śrīṁ klīṁ namo bhagavati māheśvari
annapūrṇe dhūpaṁ samarpayāmi

Oṁ Spirit of the Forest, from you is produced the most excellent of scents. The scent most pleasing to all the Gods, that scent we request you to accept. The Infinite beyond Conception, Wisdom, Māyā, the perfection of peace in the mind and in the heart, the cause of union between the gross body and causal bodies of existence, I bow to the respected Supreme Goddess, She who is full, complete and perfect in food and grains with the offering of fragrant scent.

ārātrikam

ॐ चन्द्रादित्यौ च धरणी विद्युदग्निस्तथैव च ।

त्वमेव सर्वज्योतीषिं आरात्रिकं प्रतिगृह्यताम् ॥

ॐ ऐं ह्रीं श्रीं क्लीं नमो भगवति माहेश्वरिअन्नपूर्णे आरात्रिकं समर्पयामि

oṁ candrādityau ca dharaṇī vidyudagnistathaiva ca
tvameva sarvajyotīṣiṁ ārātrikaṁ pratigṛhyatām
oṁ aiṁ hrīṁ śrīṁ klīṁ namo bhagavati māheśvari annapūrṇe ārātrikaṁ samarpayāmi

Oṁ All knowing as the Moon, the Sun and the Divine Fire, you alone are all Light, and this Light we request you to accept. The Infinite beyond Conception, Wisdom, Māyā, the perfection of peace in the mind and in the heart, the cause of union between the gross body and causal bodies of existence, I bow to the respected Supreme Goddess, She who is full, complete and perfect in food and grains with the offering of Light.

ॐ पयः पृथिव्यां पय ओषधीषु

पयो दिव्यन्तरिक्षे पयो धाः ।

पयःस्वतीः प्रदिशः सन्तु मह्यम् ॥

oṁ payaḥ pṛthivyāṁ paya oṣadhīṣu
payo divyantarikṣe payo dhāḥ
payaḥsvatīḥ pradiśaḥ santu mahyam

Oṁ Earth is a reservoir of nectar, all vegetation is a reservoir of nectar, the divine atmosphere is a reservoir of nectar, and also above. May all perceptions shine forth with the sweet taste of nectar for us.

ॐ अग्निर्देवता वातो देवता सूर्यो देवता चन्द्रमा देवता वसवो देवता रुद्रो देवता ऽदित्या देवता मरुतो देवता विश्वे देवा देवता बृहस्पतिर्देवतेन्द्रो देवता वरुणो देवता ॥

oṁ agnirdevatā vāto devatā sūryo devatā candramā devatā vasavo devatā rudro devatā-dityā devatā maruto devatā viśve devā devatā bṛhaspatirdevatendro devatā varuṇo devatā

Oṁ The Divine Fire (Light of Purity) is the shining God, the Wind is the shining God, the Sun (Light of Wisdom) is the shining God, the Moon (Lord of Devotion) is the shining God, the Protectors of the Wealth are the shining Gods, the Relievers of Sufferings are the shining Gods, the Sons of the Light are the shining Gods; the Emancipated Seers (Maruts) are the shining Gods, the Universal Shining Gods are the shining Gods, the Guru of the Gods is the shining God, the Ruler of the Gods is the shining God, the Lord of Waters is the shining God.

ॐ भूर्भुवः स्वः ।
तत् सवितुर्वरेण्यम् भर्गो देवस्य धीमहि ।
धियो यो नः प्रचोदयात् ॥

oṁ bhūr bhuvaḥ svaḥ
tat savitur vareṇyam bhargo devasya dhīmahi
dhiyo yo naḥ pracodayāt

Oṁ the Infinite Beyond Conception, the gross body, the subtle body and the causal body; we meditate upon that Light of Wisdom that is the Supreme Wealth of the Gods. May it grant to us increase in our meditations.

ॐ भूः

oṁ bhūḥ
oṁ the gross body

ॐ भुवः

oṁ bhuvaḥ
oṁ the subtle body

ॐ स्वः

oṁ svaḥ
oṁ the causal body

ॐ महः

oṁ mahaḥ
oṁ the great body of existence

ॐ जनः

oṁ janaḥ
oṁ the body of knowledge

ॐ तपः

oṁ tapaḥ
oṁ the body of light

ॐ सत्यं

oṁ satyaṁ
oṁ the body of Truth

ॐ तत् सवितुर्वरेण्यम् भर्गो देवस्य धीमहि ।
धियो यो नः प्रचोदयात् ॥

oṁ tat savitur vareṇyam bhargo devasya dhīmahi dhiyo yo naḥ pracodayāt

Oṁ We meditate upon that Light of Wisdom that is the Supreme Wealth of the Gods. May it grant to us increase in our meditations.

ॐ आपो ज्योतीरसोमृतं ब्रह्म भूर्भुवस्स्वरोम् ॥

oṁ āpo jyotīrasomṛtaṁ brahma bhūrbhuvassvarom

Oṁ May the divine waters luminous with the nectar of immortality of Supreme Divinity fill the earth, the atmosphere and the heavens.

ॐ मां माले महामाये सर्वशक्तिस्वरूपिणि ।
चतुर्वर्गस्त्वयि न्यस्तस्तस्मान्मे सिद्धिदा भव ॥

oṁ māṁ māle mahāmāye sarvaśaktisvarūpiṇi catur vargas tvayi nyastas tasmān me siddhidā bhava

Oṁ My Rosary, The Great Measurement of Consciousness, containing all energy within as your intrinsic nature, give to me the attainment of your Perfection, fulfilling the four objectives of life.

ॐ अविघ्नं कुरु माले त्वं गृह्णामि दक्षिणे करे ।
जपकाले च सिद्ध्यर्थं प्रसीद मम सिद्धये ॥

oṁ avighnaṁ kuru māle tvaṁ gṛhṇāmi dakṣiṇe kare japakāle ca siddhyarthaṁ prasīda mama siddhaye

Oṁ Rosary, You please remove all obstacles. I hold you in my right hand. At the time of recitation be pleased with me. Allow me to attain the Highest Perfection.

ॐ अक्षमालाधिपतये सुसिद्धिं देहि देहि सर्वमन्त्रार्थसाधिनि
साधय साधय सर्वसिद्धिं परिकल्पय परिकल्पय मे स्वाहा ॥

oṁ akṣa mālā dhipataye susiddhiṁ dehi dehi sarva mantrārtha sādhini sādhaya sādhaya sarva siddhiṁ parikalpaya parikalpaya me svāhā

Oṁ Rosary of rudrākṣa seeds, my Lord, give to me excellent attainment. Give to me, give to me. Illuminate the meanings of all mantras, illuminate, illuminate! Fashion me with all excellent attainments, fashion me! I am One with God!

एते गन्धपुष्पे ॐ गं गणपतये नमः

ete gandhapuṣpe oṁ gaṁ gaṇapataye namaḥ
With these scented flowers oṁ we bow to the Lord of Wisdom, Lord of the Multitudes.

एते गन्धपुष्पे ॐ आदित्यादिनवग्रहेभ्यो नमः

ete gandhapuṣpe oṁ ādityādi navagrahebhyo namaḥ
With these scented flowers oṁ we bow to the Sun, the Light of Wisdom, along with the nine planets.

एते गन्धपुष्पे ॐ शिवादिपञ्चदेवताभ्यो नमः

ete gandhapuṣpe oṁ śivādipañcadevatābhyo namaḥ
With these scented flowers oṁ we bow to Śiva, the Consciousness of Infinite Goodness, along with the five primary deities (Śiva, Śakti, Viṣṇu, Gaṇeśa, Sūrya).

एते गन्धपुष्पे ॐ इन्द्रादिदशदिक्पालेभ्यो नमः

ete gandhapuṣpe oṁ indrādi daśadikpālebhyo namaḥ
With these scented flowers oṁ we bow to Indra, the Ruler of the Pure, along with the Ten Protectors of the ten directions.

एते गन्धपुष्पे ॐ मत्स्यादिदशावतारेभ्यो नमः

ete gandhapuṣpe oṁ matsyādi daśāvatārebhyo namaḥ
With these scented flowers oṁ we bow to Viṣṇu, the Fish, along with the Ten Incarnations that He assumed.

एते गन्धपुष्पे ॐ प्रजापतये नमः

ete gandhapuṣpe oṁ prajāpataye namaḥ

With these scented flowers oṁ we bow to the Lord of All Created Beings.

एते गन्धपुष्पे ॐ नमो नारायणाय नमः

ete gandhapuṣpe oṁ namo nārāyaṇāya namaḥ

With these scented flowers oṁ we bow to the Perfect Perception of Consciousness.

एते गन्धपुष्पे ॐ सर्वेभ्यो देवेभ्यो नमः

ete gandhapuṣpe oṁ sarvebhyo devebhyo namaḥ

With these scented flowers oṁ we bow to All the Gods.

एते गन्धपुष्पे ॐ सर्वाभ्यो देवीभ्यो नमः

ete gandhapuṣpe oṁ sarvābhyo devībhyo namaḥ

With these scented flowers oṁ we bow to All the Goddesses.

एते गन्धपुष्पे ॐ श्री गुरवे नमः

ete gandhapuṣpe oṁ śrī gurave namaḥ

With these scented flowers oṁ we bow to the Guru.

एते गन्धपुष्पे ॐ ब्राह्मणेभ्यो नमः

ete gandhapuṣpe oṁ brāhmaṇebhyo namaḥ

With these scented flowers oṁ we bow to All Knowers of Wisdom.

Tie a piece of string around right middle finger or wrist.

ॐ कुशासने स्थितो ब्रह्मा कुशे चैव जनार्दनः ।
कुशे ह्याकाशवद् विष्णुः कुशासन नमोऽस्तु ते ॥

oṁ kuśāsane sthito brahmā kuśe caiva janārdanaḥ
kuśe hyākāśavad viṣṇuḥ kuśāsana namo-stu te

Brahmā is in the shining light (or kuśa grass), in the shining light resides Janārdana, the Lord of Beings. The Supreme all-pervading Consciousness, Viṣṇu, resides in the shining light. Oh Repository of the shining light, we bow down to you, the seat of kuśa grass.

आचमन
ācamana

ॐ केशवाय नमः स्वाहा

oṁ keśavāya namaḥ svāhā

Oṁ We bow to the one of beautiful hair.

ॐ माधवाय नमः स्वाहा

oṁ mādhavāya namaḥ svāhā

Oṁ We bow to the one who is always sweet.

ॐ गोविन्दाय नमः स्वाहा

oṁ govindāya namaḥ svāhā

Oṁ We bow to He who is one-pointed light.

ॐ विष्णुः ॐ विष्णुः ॐ विष्णुः

oṁ viṣṇuḥ oṁ viṣṇuḥ oṁ viṣṇuḥ

Oṁ Consciousness, oṁ Consciousness, oṁ Consciousness.

ॐ तत् विष्णोः परमं पदम् सदा पश्यन्ति सूरयः ।
दिवीव चक्षुराततम् ॥

oṁ tat viṣṇoḥ paramaṁ padam sadā paśyanti sūrayaḥ
divīva cakṣurā tatam

Oṁ That Consciousness of the highest station, who always sees the Light of Wisdom, give us Divine Eyes.

ॐ तद् विप्र स पिपानोव जुविग्रन्सो सोमिन्द्रते ।
विष्णुः तत् परमं पदम् ॥

oṁ tad vipra sa pipānova juvigranso somindrate
viṣṇuḥ tat paramaṁ padam

Oṁ That twice-born teacher who is always thirsty for accepting the nectar of devotion, Oh Consciousness, you are in that highest station.

ॐ अपवित्रः पवित्रो वा सर्वावस्थां गतोऽपि वा ।
यः स्मरेत् पुण्डरीकाक्षं स बाह्याभ्यन्तरः शुचिः ॥

oṁ apavitraḥ pavitro vā sarvāvasthāṁ gato-pi vā
yaḥ smaret puṇḍarīkākṣaṁ sa bāhyābhyantaraḥ śuciḥ

Oṁ The Impure and the Pure reside within all objects. Who remembers the lotus-eyed Consciousness is conveyed to radiant beauty.

ॐ सर्वमङ्गलमाङ्गल्यम् वरेण्यम् वरदं शुभं ।
नारायणं नमस्कृत्य सर्वकर्माणि कारयेत् ॥

oṁ sarva maṅgala māṅgalyam
vareṇyam varadaṁ śubhaṁ
nārāyaṇaṁ namaskṛtya sarvakarmāṇi kārayet

Oṁ All the Welfare of all Welfare, the highest blessing of Purity and Illumination, with the offering of respect we bow down to the Supreme Consciousness who is the actual performer of all action.

ॐ सूर्य्यश्चमेति मन्त्रस्य ब्रह्मा ऋषिः प्रकृतिश्छन्दः आपो देवता आचमने विनियोगः ॥

oṁ sūryyaścameti mantrasya brahmā ṛṣiḥ
prakṛtiśchandaḥ āpo devatā ācamane viniyogaḥ

Oṁ these are the mantras of the Light of Wisdom, the Creative Capacity is the Seer, Nature is the meter, the divine flow of waters is the deity, being applied in washing the hands and rinsing the mouth.

Draw the following yantra with some drops of water and/or sandal paste at the front of your seat. Place a flower on the bindu in the middle.

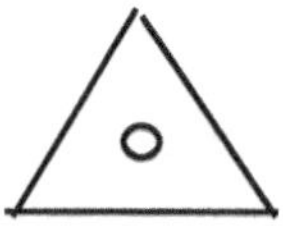

ॐ आसनस्य मन्त्रस्य मेरुपृष्ठ ऋषिः सुतलं छन्दः कूर्म्मो देवता आसनोपवेशने विनियोगः ॥

oṁ āsanasya mantrasya merupṛṣṭha ṛṣiḥ sutalaṁ chandaḥ kūrmmo devatā āsanopaveśane viniyogaḥ

Oṁ Introducing the mantras of the Purification of the seat. The Seer is He whose back is Straight, the meter is of very beautiful form, the tortoise who supports the Earth is the deity. These mantras are applied to make the seat free from obstructions.

एते गन्धपुष्पे ॐ ह्रीं आधारशक्तये कमलासनाय नमः ॥

ete gandhapuṣpe oṁ hrīṁ ādhāraśaktaye kamalāsanāya namaḥ

With these scented flowers oṁ hrīṁ we bow to the Primal Energy situated in this lotus seat.

ॐ पृथ्वि त्वया धृता लोका देवि त्वं विष्णुना धृता ।
त्वञ्च धारय मां नित्यं पवित्रं कुरु चासनम् ॥

oṁ pṛthvi tvayā dhṛtā lokā devi tvaṁ viṣṇunā dhṛtā tvañca dhāraya māṁ nityaṁ pavitraṁ kuru cāsanam

Oṁ Earth! You support the realms of the Goddess. You are supported by the Supreme Consciousness. Also bear me eternally and make pure this seat.

ॐ गुरुभ्यो नमः

oṁ gurubhyo namaḥ
Oṁ I bow to the Guru.

ॐ परमगुरुभ्यो नमः

oṁ paramagurubhyo namaḥ
Oṁ I bow to the Guru's Guru.

ॐ परापरगुरुभ्यो नमः

oṁ parāparagurubhyo namaḥ
Oṁ I bow to the Gurus of the lineage.

ॐ परमेष्ठिगुरुभ्यो नमः

oṁ parameṣṭhigurubhyo namaḥ
Oṁ I bow to the Supreme Gurus.

ॐ गं गणेशाय नमः

oṁ gaṁ gaṇeśāya namaḥ
Oṁ I bow to the Lord of Wisdom.

ॐ अनन्ताय नमः

oṁ anantāya namaḥ
Oṁ I bow to the Infinite One.

ॐ ऐं ह्रीं क्लीं चामुण्डायै विच्चे

oṁ aiṁ hrīṁ klīṁ cāmuṇḍāyai vicce
Oṁ Creation, Circumstance, Transformation are known by Consciousness.

ॐ नमः शिवाय

oṁ namaḥ śivāya
Oṁ I bow to the Consciousness of Infinite Goodness.

Clap hands three times and snap fingers in the ten directions (N S E W NE SW NW SE UP DOWN) repeating

ॐ ऐं ह्रीं श्रीं क्लीं नमो भगवति माहेश्वरिअन्नपूर्णे

oṁ aiṁ hrīṁ śrīṁ klīṁ namo bhagavati māheśvari annapūrṇe

Oṁ The Infinite beyond Conception, Wisdom, Māyā, the perfection of peace in the mind and in the heart, the cause of union between the gross body and causal bodies of existence, I bow to the respected Supreme Goddess, She who is full, complete and perfect in food and grains.

सङ्कल्प

saṅkalpa

विष्णुः ॐ तत् सत् । ॐ अद्य जम्बूद्वीपे ( ) देशे ( ) प्रदेशे ( ) नगरे ( ) मन्दिरे ( ) मासे ( ) पक्षे ( ) तिथौ ( ) गोत्र श्री ( ) कृतैतत् श्रीमाहेश्वरिअन्नपूर्णा कामः पूजाकर्माहं श्रीअन्नपूर्णा सहस्र नाम करिष्ये ॥

viṣṇuḥ oṁ tat sat oṁ adya jambūdvīpe (Country) deśe (State) pradeśe (City) nagare (Name of house or temple) mandire (month) māse (śukla or kṛṣṇa) pakṣe (name of day) tithau (name of) gotra śrī (your name) kṛtaitat śrī māheśvari annapūrṇā kāmaḥ pūjakarmāhaṁ śrī annapūrṇā sahasra nāma kariṣye

The Consciousness That Pervades All, oṁ That is Truth. Presently, on the Planet Earth, Country of (Name), State of (Name), City of (Name), in the Temple of (Name), (Name of Month) Month, (Bright or Dark) fortnight, (Name of Day) Day, (Name of Sādhu Family), Śrī (Your Name) is performing the worship for the satisfaction of the respected Supreme Goddess, She who is full, complete and perfect in food and grains by reciting the thousand names.

ॐ यज्जाग्रतो दूरमुदेति दैवं तदु सुप्तस्य तथैवैति ।
दूरङ्गमं ज्योतिषां ज्योतिरेकं तन्मे मनः शिवसङ्कल्पमस्तु ॥

oṁ yajjāgrato dūramudeti
daivaṁ tadu suptasya tathaivaiti
dūraṅgamaṁ jyotiṣāṁ jyotirekaṁ
tanme manaḥ śiva saṅkalpamastu

Oṁ May our waking consciousness replace pain and suffering with divinity as also our awareness when asleep. Far extending be our radiant aura of light, filling our minds with light. May that be the firm determination of the Consciousness of Infinite Goodness.

या गुङ्गूर्या सिनीवाली या राका या सरस्वती ।
ईन्द्राणीमह्व ऊतये वरुणानीं स्वस्तये ॥

yā guṅgūryā sinīvālī yā rākā yā sarasvatī
īndrāṇīmahva ūtaye varuṇānīṁ svastaye

May that Goddess who wears the Moon of Devotion protect the children of Devotion. May that Goddess of All-Pervading Knowledge protect us. May the Energy of the Rule of the Pure rise up. Oh Energy of Equilibrium grant us the highest prosperity.

ॐ स्वस्ति न इन्द्रो वृद्धश्रवाः स्वस्ति नः पूषा विश्ववेदाः ।
स्वस्ति नस्तार्क्ष्यो अरिष्टनेमिः स्वस्ति नो बृहस्पतिर्दधातु ॥

oṁ svasti na indro vṛddhaśravāḥ
svasti naḥ pūṣā viśvavedāḥ
svasti nastārkṣyo ariṣṭanemiḥ
svasti no bṛhaspatirdadhātu

Oṁ The Ultimate Prosperity to us, Oh Rule of the Pure, who perceives all that changes; the Ultimate Prosperity to us, Searchers for Truth, Knowers of the Universe; the Ultimate Prosperity to us, Oh Divine Being of Light, keep us safe; the

Ultimate Prosperity to us, Oh Spirit of All-Pervading Delight, grant that to us.

ॐ गणानां त्वा गणपति हवामहे
प्रियाणां त्वा प्रियपति हवामहे
निधीनां त्वा निधिपति हवामहे वसो मम ।
आहमजानि गर्ब्भधमा त्वमजासि गर्ब्भधम् ॥

oṁ gaṇānāṁ tvā gaṇapati guṁ havāmahe
priyāṇāṁ tvā priyapati guṁ havāmahe
nidhīnāṁ tvā nidhipati guṁ havāmahe vaso mama
āhamajāni garbbhadhamā tvamajāsi garbbhadham

Oṁ We invoke you with offerings, Oh Lord of the Multitudes; we invoke you with offerings, Oh Lord of Love; we invoke you with offerings, Oh Guardian of the Treasure. Sit within me, giving birth to the realm of the Gods within me; yes, giving birth to the realm of the Gods within me.

ॐ गणानां त्वा गणपति हवामहे
कविं कवीनामुपमश्रवस्तमम् ।
ज्येष्ठराजं ब्रह्मणां ब्रह्मणस्पत
आ नः शृण्वन्नूतिभिः सीद सादनम् ॥

oṁ gaṇānāṁ tvā gaṇapati guṁ havāmahe
kaviṁ kavīnāmupamaśravastamam
jyeṣṭharājaṁ brahmaṇāṁ brahmaṇaspata
ā naḥ śṛṇvannūtibhiḥ sīda sādanam

Oṁ We invoke you with offerings, Oh Lord of the Multitudes, Seer among Seers, of unspeakable grandeur. Oh Glorious King, Lord of the Knowers of Wisdom, come speedily hearing our supplications and graciously take your seat amidst our assembly.

ॐ अदितिर्द्यौरदितिरन्तरिक्षमदितिर्माता स पिता

स पुत्रः । विश्वे देवा अदितिः पञ्च जना

अदितिर्जातमदितिर्जनित्वम् ॥

oṁ aditir dyauraditirantarikṣamaditirmātā sa pitā sa putraḥ
viśve devā aditiḥ pañca janā
aditirjātamaditirjanitvam

Oṁ The Mother of Enlightenment pervades the heavens; the Mother of Enlightenment pervades the atmosphere; the Mother of Enlightenment pervades Mother and Father and child. All Gods of the Universe are pervaded by the Mother, the five forms of living beings, all Life. The Mother of Enlightenment, She is to be known.

ॐ त्वं स्त्रीस्त्वं पुमानसि त्वं कुमार अत वा कुमारी ।

त्वं जिर्नो वन्देन वञ्चसि त्वं जातो भवसि विश्वतोमुखः ॥

oṁ tvaṁ strīstvaṁ pumānasi
tvaṁ kumāra ata vā kumārī
tvaṁ jirno vandena vañcasi
tvaṁ jāto bhavasi viśvatomukhaḥ

Oṁ You are Female, you are Male; you are a young boy, you are a young girl. You are the word of praise by which we are singing; you are all creation existing as the mouth of the universe.

ॐ श्रीश्च ते लक्ष्मीश्च पत्न्यावहोरात्रे पार्श्वे नक्षत्राणि

रूपमश्विनौ व्यात्तम् । इष्णं निषाणामुं म ऽइषाण सर्वलोकं

म ऽइषाण ॥

oṁ śrīśca te lakṣmīśca patnyāvahorātre pārśve nakṣatrāṇi rūpamaśvinau vyāttam
iṣṇaṁ niṣāṇāmuṁ ma -iṣāṇa sarvalokaṁ ma-iṣāṇa

Oṁ the Highest Respect to you, Goal of all Existence, wife of the full and complete night (the Unknowable One), at whose sides are the stars, and who has the form of the relentless search for Truth. Oh Supreme Divinity, Supreme Divinity, my Supreme Divinity, all existence is my Supreme Divinity.

ॐ अम्बेऽम्बिकेऽम्बालिके न मा नयति कश्चन ।
ससस्त्यश्वकः सुभद्रिकां काम्पीलवासिनीम् ॥

oṁ ambe-ambike-mbālike na mā nayati kaścana
sasastyaśvakaḥ subhadrikāṁ kāmpīlavāsinīm

Oṁ Mother of the Perceivable Universe, Mother of the Conceivable Universe, Mother of the Universe of Intuitive Vision, lead me to that True Existence. As excellent crops (or grains) are harvested, so may I be taken to reside with the Infinite Consciousness.

ॐ शान्ता द्यौः शान्तापृथिवी शान्तमिदमुर्वन्तरिक्षम् ।
शान्ता उदन्वतिरापः शान्ताः नः शान्त्वोषधीः ॥

oṁ śāntā dyauḥ śāntā pṛthivī śāntam
idamurvantarikṣam
śāntā udanvatirāpaḥ śāntāḥ naḥ śāntvoṣadhīḥ

Oṁ Peace in the heavens, Peace on the earth, Peace upwards and permeating the atmosphere; Peace upwards, over, on all sides and further; Peace to us, Peace to all vegetation;

ॐ शान्तानि पूर्वरूपाणि शान्तं नोऽस्तु कृताकृतम् ।
शान्तं भूतं च भव्यं च सर्वमेव शमस्तु नः ॥

oṁ śāntāni pūrva rūpāṇi śāntaṁ no-stu kṛtākṛtam
śāntaṁ bhūtaṁ ca bhavyaṁ ca
sarvameva śamastu naḥ

Oṁ Peace to all that has form, Peace to all causes and effects; Peace to all existence, and to all intensities of reality, including all and everything; Peace be to us.

ॐ पृथिवी शान्तिरन्तरिक्षं शान्तिर्द्यौः
शान्तिरापः शान्तिरोषधयः शान्तिः वनस्पतयः शान्तिर्विश्वे
मे देवाः शान्तिः सर्वे मे देवाः शान्तिर्ब्रह्म शान्तिरापः शान्तिः
सर्वं शान्तिरेधि शान्तिः शान्तिः सर्व शान्तिः सा मा शान्तिः
शान्तिभिः ॥

oṁ pṛthivī śāntir antarikṣaṁ śāntir dyauḥ
śāntir āpaḥ śāntir oṣadhayaḥ śāntiḥ vanaspatayaḥ
śāntir viśve me devāḥ śāntiḥ sarve me devāḥ śāntir
brahma śāntirāpaḥ śāntiḥ sarvaṁ śāntiredhi śāntiḥ
śāntiḥ sarva śāntiḥ sā mā śāntiḥ śāntibhiḥ

Oṁ Let the earth be at Peace, the atmosphere be at Peace, the heavens be filled with Peace. Even further may Peace extend, Peace be to waters, Peace to all vegetation, Peace to All Gods of the Universe, Peace to All Gods within us, Peace to Creative Consciousness, Peace to Brilliant Light, Peace to All, Peace to Everything, Peace, Peace, altogether Peace, equally Peace, by means of Peace.

ताभिः शान्तिभिः सर्वशान्तिभिः समया मोहं यदिह घोरं
यदिह क्रूरं यदिह पापं तच्छान्तं तच्छिवं सर्वमेव समस्तु
नः ॥

tābhiḥ śāntibhiḥ sarva śāntibhiḥ samayā mohaṁ
yadiha ghoraṁ yadiha krūraṁ yadiha pāpaṁ
tacchāntaṁ tacchivaṁ sarvameva samastu naḥ

Thus by means of Peace, altogether one with the means of Peace, Ignorance is eliminated, Violence is eradicated, Improper Conduct is eradicated, Confusion (sin) is eradicated, all that is, is at Peace, all that is perceived, each and everything, altogether for us,

ॐ शान्तिः शान्तिः शान्तिः ॥

oṁ śāntiḥ śāntiḥ śāntiḥ

Oṁ Peace, Peace, Peace

ॐ ह्रीं अन्नपूर्णायै स्वाहा

oṁ hrīṁ annapūrṇāyai svāhā

The Infinite Beyond Conception, Māyā, She who is full, complete and perfect in food and grains, I am One with God

ॐ ऐं ह्रीं श्रीं क्लीं नमो भगवति माहेश्वरिअन्नपूर्णे

oṁ aiṁ hrīṁ śrīṁ klīṁ namo bhagavati māheśvari annapūrṇe

The Infinite Beyond Conception, Wisdom, Māyā, the perfection of peace in the mind and in the heart, the cause of union between the gross body and causal bodies of existence, I bow to the respected Supreme Goddess, She who is full, complete and perfect in food and grains

ॐ भगवत्यै विद्महे माहेश्वर्यै च धीमहि ।
तन्नो अन्नपूर्णा प्रचोदयात् ॥

**oṁ bhagavatyai vidmahe māheśvaryai ca dhīmahi |
tanno annapūrṇā pracodayāt ||**

Oṁ We know the Supreme Goddess, contemplate the Great Supreme Divinity. May Annapūrṇā grant us increase.

विनियोगः

viniyogaḥ

ॐ अस्य श्रीअन्नपूर्णासिहस्रनाम-स्तोत्र मंत्रस्य श्रीभगवान् सदाशिवऋषिः अनुष्टुप् - छन्दः ॐ भगवती श्रीमन्महा श्रीअन्नपूर्णा देवता हलो बीजम् स्वराशशक्तिः जीवोबीजम् बुद्धि-शशक्तिः उदानो बीजं सुशुम्नानाडी सरस्वती शक्तिः धर्मार्थकाममोक्षार्थे जपे विनियोगः ।

oṁ asya śrīannapūrṇāsahasranāma-stotra maṁtrasya śrībhagavān sadāśiva ṛṣiḥ anuṣṭup - chandaḥ oṁ bhagavatī śrīmanmahā śrīannapūrṇā devatā halo bījāṁ, svarāśaśaktiḥ jīvobījam, buddhi-śaśaktiḥ udāno bījaṁ, suśumnānāḍī, sarasvatī śaktiḥ dharmārthakāmamokṣārthe jape viniyogaḥ |

Oṁ Presenting the song of mantras containing one thousand names of the respected Supreme Goddess, She who is full, complete and perfect in food and grains, the Eternal Śiva is the seer, anuṣṭup is the meter (32 syllables to the verse), oṁ the Supreme Goddess, the greatly respected Annapūrṇā is the deity, halo is the seed, melody is the energy, the individual soul is the seed, intelligence is the energy, the rising breath is the seed, the suśumnā, the subtle canal of the spine, is the channel through which energy flows, Sarasvati, the Goddess of Knowledge, is the energy, for the perfection of the ideals of perfection, the resources necessary to attain those ideals and liberation, this system is applied in recitation.

श्री अन्नपूर्णा सहस्र नामावली

śrī annapūrṇā sahasra nāmāvalī

The Thousand Names of She who is full,
complete and perfect in food and grains

- 1 -

ॐ अन्नपूर्णायै स्वाहा

oṁ annapūrṇāyai svāhā

She who is full, complete and perfect in food and grains

- 2 -

ॐ अन्नदात्र्यै स्वाहा

oṁ annadātryai svāhā

She who is the creator of food

- 3 -

ॐ अन्नराशिकृताऽलयायै स्वाहा

oṁ annarāśikṛtā-layāyai svāhā

She who creates and dissolves the world of food and grains

- 4 -

ॐ अन्नदायै स्वाहा

oṁ annadāyai svāhā

She who is the giver of food and grains

- 5 -

ॐ अन्नरूपायै स्वाहा

oṁ annarūpāyai svāhā

She who is the form of food and grains

- 6 -

ॐ अन्नदानरतोत्सवायै स्वाहा

oṁ annadānaratotsavāyai svāhā

She who is the festival of giving food and grains

- 7 -

ॐ अन्नतायै स्वाहा

oṁ annatāyai svāhā

She who gives the energy of food and grains

- 8 -

ॐ अनन्ताक्ष्यै स्वाहा

oṁ anantākṣyai svāhā

She who has infinite eyes

- 9 -

ॐ अनन्तगुणशालिन्यै स्वाहा

oṁ anantaguṇaśālinyai svāhā

She who is the repository of infinite qualities

- 10 -

ॐ अमृतायै स्वाहा

oṁ amṛtāyai svāhā

She who is the nectar of immortal bliss

- 11 -

ॐ अच्युतप्राणायै स्वाहा

oṁ acyutaprāṇāyai svāhā

She who is the life force of the imperishable

- 12 -

ॐ अच्युतानन्दकारिण्यै स्वाहा

oṁ acyutānandakāriṇyai svāhā
She who is the cause of imperishable bliss

- 13 -

ॐ अव्यक्तायै स्वाहा

oṁ avyaktāyai svāhā
She who is indivisible

- 14 -

ॐ अनन्तमहिमायै स्वाहा

oṁ anantamahimāyai svāhā
She who has infinite greatness

- 15 -

ॐ अनन्तस्य कुलेश्वर्यै स्वाहा

oṁ anantasya kuleśvaryai svāhā
She who is the supreme sovereign of the infinite family

- 16 -

ॐ अब्धिस्थायै स्वाहा

oṁ abdhisthāyai svāhā
She who resides in the infinite ocean

- 17 -

ॐ अब्धिशयनायै स्वाहा

oṁ abdhiśayanāyai svāhā
She who rests in the infinite ocean

- 18-

ॐ अब्धिजायै स्वाहा

oṁ abdhijāyai svāhā
She who is born in the infinite ocean

- 19 -

ॐ अब्धिनन्दिन्यै स्वाहा

oṁ abdhinandinyai svāhā
She who is the bliss of the infinite ocean

- 20 -

ॐ अब्जस्थायै स्वाहा

oṁ abjasthāyai svāhā
She who is situated in the infinite ocean

- 21 -

ॐ अब्जनिलयायै स्वाहा

oṁ abjanilayāyai svāhā
She who is hidden in the infinite ocean

- 22 -

ॐ अब्जजायै स्वाहा

oṁ abjajāyai svāhā
She who gives birth to the infinite ocean

- 23 -

ॐ अब्जभूषणायै स्वाहा

oṁ abjabhūṣaṇāyai svāhā
She who is the ornament of the infinite ocean

- 24 -

ॐ अब्जाभायै स्वाहा

oṁ abjābhāyai svāhā

She who makes the infinite ocean shine

- 25 -

ॐ अब्जहस्तायै स्वाहा

oṁ abjahastāyai svāhā

She who holds the infinite ocean in her hands

- 26 -

ॐ अब्जपत्रशुभेक्षणायै स्वाहा

oṁ abjapatraśubhekṣaṇāyai svāhā

She who is the beautiful container of the infinite ocean

- 27 -

ॐ अब्जासनायै स्वाहा

oṁ abjāsanāyai svāhā

She who sits within the infinite ocean

- 28 -

ॐ अनन्तात्ममायै स्वाहा

oṁ anantātmamāyai svāhā

She who is the manifestation of the infinite soul

- 29 -

ॐ अग्निस्थायै स्वाहा

oṁ agnisthāyai svāhā

She who is situated in fire

- 30 -

ॐ अग्निरूपिण्यै स्वाहा

oṁ agnirūpiṇyai svāhā
She who is the form of fire

- 31 -

ॐ अग्निजायायै स्वाहा

oṁ agnijāyāyai svāhā
She who gives birth to fire

- 32 -

ॐ अग्निमुख्यै स्वाहा

oṁ agnimukhyai svāhā
She who is the mouth of fire

- 33 -

ॐ अग्निकुण्डकृतालयायै स्वाहा

oṁ agnikuṇḍakṛtālayāyai svāhā
She who creates and destroys the fire in its sacrificial place

- 34 -

ॐ अकारायै स्वाहा

oṁ akārāyai svāhā
She who is the first letter A

- 35 -

ॐ अग्निमात्रे स्वाहा

oṁ agnimātre svāhā
She who is the mother of fire

- 36 -

ॐ अजयायै स्वाहा

oṁ ajayāyai svāhā
She who is unborn

- 37 -

ॐ अदितिनन्दिन्यै स्वाहा

oṁ aditinandinyai svāhā
She who is the representative of the one without duality

- 38 -

ॐ आद्यायै स्वाहा

oṁ ādyāyai svāhā
She who is the foremost

- 39 -

ॐ आदित्यसङ्काशायै स्वाहा

oṁ ādityasaṅkāśāyai svāhā
She who is the visible form of the one without duality

- 40 -

ॐ आत्मज्ञायै स्वाहा

oṁ ātmajñāyai svāhā
She who is the wisdom of the soul

- 41 -

ॐ आत्मगोचरायै स्वाहा

oṁ ātmagocarāyai svāhā
She who moves the light of the soul

- 42 -

ॐ आत्मसुवे स्वाहा

oṁ ātmasuve svāhā
She who is the excellence of the soul

- 43 -

ॐ आत्मदयितायै स्वाहा

oṁ ātmadayitāyai svāhā
She who is the giver of the soul

- 44 -

ॐ आधारायै स्वाहा

oṁ ādhārāyai svāhā
She who is the primary support

- 45 -

ॐ आत्मरूपिण्यै स्वाहा

oṁ ātmarūpiṇyai svāhā
She who is the form of the soul

- 46 -

ॐ आशायै स्वाहा

oṁ āśāyai svāhā
She who is hope

- 47 -

ॐ आकाशपद्मस्थायै स्वाहा

oṁ ākāśapadmasthāyai svāhā
She who resides in a lotus in the ether

- 48 -

ॐ अवकाशस्वरूपिण्यै स्वाहा

oṁ avakāśasvarūpiṇyai svāhā

She who is the intrinsic nature of manifestation

- 49 -

ॐ आशापूर्यै स्वाहा

oṁ āśāpūryai svāhā

She who fulfills all desires

- 50 -

ॐ अगाधायै स्वाहा

oṁ agādhāyai svāhā

She who is unfathomable

- 51 -

ॐ अणिमादिसुसेवितायै स्वाहा

oṁ aṇimādisusevitāyai svāhā

She who is served by those who have siddhis such as being able to become small

- 52 -

ॐ अम्बिकायै स्वाहा

oṁ ambikāyai svāhā

She who is the mother of perceivable existence

- 53 -

ॐ अबलायै स्वाहा

oṁ abalāyai svāhā

She who is weak or feeble

\- 54 -

ॐ अम्बायै स्वाहा

oṁ ambāyai svāhā
She who is the mother of all

\- 55 -

ॐ अनाद्यायै स्वाहा

oṁ anādyāyai svāhā
She who is beyond vibrations

\- 56 -

ॐ अयोनिजायै स्वाहा

oṁ ayonijāyai svāhā
She who is born without a womb

\- 57 -

ॐ अनिशायै स्वाहा

oṁ aniśāyai svāhā
She who continues incessantly

\- 58 -

ॐ ईशिकायै स्वाहा

oṁ īśikāyai svāhā
She who is the master

\- 59 -

ॐ ईशायै स्वाहा

oṁ īśāyai svāhā
She who is the ruler

- 60 -

ॐ ईशान्यै स्वाहा

oṁ īśānyai svāhā

She who possesses

- 61 -

ॐ ईश्वरप्रियायै स्वाहा

oṁ īśvarapriyāyai svāhā

She who is the beloved of the supreme

- 62 -

ॐ ईश्वर्यै स्वाहा

oṁ īśvaryai svāhā

She who is the supreme

- 63 -

ॐ ईश्वरप्राणायै स्वाहा

oṁ īśvaraprāṇāyai svāhā

She who is the life of the supreme

- 64 -

ॐ ईश्वरानन्ददायिन्यै स्वाहा

oṁ īśvarānandadāyinyai svāhā

She who is the giver of bliss to the supreme

- 65 -

ॐ इन्द्राण्यै स्वाहा

oṁ indrāṇyai svāhā

She who is the energy of the rule of the pure

- 66 -

ॐ इन्द्रदयितायै स्वाहा

oṁ indradayitāyai svāhā

She who gives lordship

- 67 -

ॐ इन्द्रसुवे स्वाहा

oṁ indrasuve svāhā

She who is the excellent rule of the pure

- 68 -

ॐ इन्द्रपालिन्यै स्वाहा

oṁ indrapālinyai svāhā

She who protects the rule of the pure

- 69 -

ॐ इन्दिरायै स्वाहा

oṁ indirāyai svāhā

She who controls the goal

- 70 -

ॐ इन्द्रभगिन्यै स्वाहा

oṁ indrabhaginyai svāhā

She who is the part of the rule of the pure

- 71 -

ॐ इन्द्रियायै स्वाहा

oṁ indriyāyai svāhā

She who is all the senses

- 72 -

ॐ इन्दुभूषणायै स्वाहा

oṁ indubhūṣaṇāyai svāhā

She who is the illumination of the moon of devotion

- 73 -

ॐ इन्दुमात्रायै स्वाहा

oṁ indumātrāyai svāhā

She who is the mother of the moon of devotion

- 74 -

ॐ इन्दुमुख्यै स्वाहा

oṁ indumukhyai svāhā

She who is the mouth of the moon of devotion

- 75 -

ॐ इन्द्रियाणां वशंकर्यै स्वाहा

oṁ indriyāṇāṁ vaśaṁkaryai svāhā

She who is the cause of the control of the senses

- 76 -

ॐ उमायै स्वाहा

oṁ umāyai svāhā

She who is the mother of circumstances

- 77 -

ॐ उमापतेः प्राणायै स्वाहा

oṁ umāpateḥ prāṇāyai svāhā

She who is the life force of the lord of the mother of circumstances

- 78 -

ॐ उड्याणपीठवासिन्यै स्वाहा

oṁ uḍyāṇapīṭhavāsinyai svāhā
She who resides in the place of rising energy

- 79 -

ॐ उत्तरज्ञायै स्वाहा

oṁ uttarajñāyai svāhā
She who is the wisdom that rises

- 80 -

ॐ उत्तराख्यायै स्वाहा

oṁ uttarākhyāyai svāhā
She who is completely superior

- 81 -

ॐ उकारायै स्वाहा

oṁ ukārāyai svāhā
She who is the letter U

- 82 -

ॐ उत्तरात्मिकायै स्वाहा

oṁ uttarātmikāyai svāhā
She who is the manifestation of the highest soul

- 83 -

ॐ ऋमात्रे स्वाहा

oṁ ṛmātre svāhā
She who is the mother of Ṛ

- 84 -

ॐ ऋभवायै स्वाहा

oṁ ṛbhavāyai svāhā

She who is the existence of Ṛ

- 85 -

ॐ ऋस्थायै स्वाहा

oṁ ṛsthāyai svāhā

She resides in Ṛ

- 86 -

ॐ ऋलृकारस्वरूपिण्यै स्वाहा

oṁ ṛḷkārasvarūpiṇyai svāhā

She who is the intrinsic nature of the letters Ṛ and Lṛ

- 87 -

ॐ ऋकारायै स्वाहा

oṁ ṛkārāyai svāhā

She who is the letter Ṛ

- 88 -

ॐ लृकारायै स्वाहा

oṁ ḷkārāyai svāhā

She who is a letter Lṛ

- 89 -

ॐ लृकारप्रीतिदायिन्यै स्वाहा

oṁ ḷkāraprītidāyinyai svāhā

She who gives the love of the letter Lṛ

- 90 -

ॐ एकायै स्वाहा

oṁ ekāyai svāhā
She who is the letter E

- 91 -

ॐ एकवीरायै स्वाहा

oṁ ekavīrāyai svāhā
She who is solely attentive to the battle

- 92 -

ॐ ऐकाररूपिण्यै स्वाहा

oṁ aikārarūpiṇyai svāhā
She who is the intrinsic nature of the letter Ai

- 93 -

ॐ ओकार्यै स्वाहा

oṁ okāryai svāhā
She who is the letter O

- 94 -

ॐ ओघरूपायै स्वाहा

oṁ ogharūpāyai svāhā
She who is the form of abundance

- 95 -

ॐ ओघत्रयसुपूजितायै स्वाहा

oṁ oghatrayasupūjitāyai svāhā
She who is the abundance that is worshipped by the inhabitants of the three worlds

- 96 -

ॐ ओघस्थायै स्वाहा

oṁ oghasthāyai svāhā
She who resides in abundance

- 97 -

ॐ ओघसंभूतायै स्वाहा

oṁ oghasaṁbhūtāyai svāhā
She who shines forth with abundance

- 98 -

ॐ ओघदात्र्यै स्वाहा

oṁ oghadātryai svāhā
She who gives abundance

- 99 -

ॐ ओघसुवे स्वाहा

oṁ oghasuve svāhā
She who is excellent abundance

- 100 -

ॐ षोडशस्वरसंभूतायै स्वाहा

oṁ ṣoḍaśasvarasaṁbhūtāyai svāhā
She who shines with the sixteen melodies

- 101 -

ॐ षोडशस्वररूपिण्यै स्वाहा

oṁ ṣoḍaśasvarūpiṇyai svāhā
She who is the intrinsic nature of the sixteen melodies

- 102 -

ॐ वर्णात्मायै स्वाहा

oṁ varṇātmāyai svāhā
She who is the manifestation of all colors, castes and creeds

- 103 -

ॐ वर्णनिलयायै स्वाहा

oṁ varṇanilayāyai svāhā
She who reposes with all colors, casts and creeds

- 104 -

ॐ शूलिन्यै स्वाहा

oṁ śūlinyai svāhā
She who holds a spear

- 105 -

ॐ वर्णमालिन्यै स्वाहा

oṁ varṇamālinyai svāhā
She who is the garland of all colors casts and creeds

- 106 -

ॐ कालरात्र्यै स्वाहा

oṁ kālarātryai svāhā
She who is the dark night of overcoming egotism

- 107 -

ॐ महारात्र्यै स्वाहा

oṁ mahārātryai svāhā
She who is the great night

- 108 -

ॐ मोहरात्र्यै स्वाहा

oṁ moharātryai svāhā
She who is the night of ignorance

- 109 -

ॐ सुलोचनायै स्वाहा

oṁ sulocanāyai svāhā
She who has beautiful eyes

- 110 -

ॐ काल्यै स्वाहा

oṁ kālyai svāhā
She who is dark

- 111 -

ॐ कपालिन्यै स्वाहा

oṁ kapālinyai svāhā
She who holds a skull

- 112 -

ॐ कृत्यायै स्वाहा

oṁ kṛtyāyai svāhā
She who is the doer

- 113 -

ॐ कलिकायै स्वाहा

oṁ kalikāyai svāhā
She who is beyond darkness

- 114 -

ॐ सिंहगामिन्यै स्वाहा

oṁ siṁhagāminyai svāhā
She who moves with a lion

- 115 -

ॐ कात्यायन्यै स्वाहा

oṁ kātyāyanyai svāhā
She who is ever pure

- 116 -

ॐ कलाधारायै स्वाहा

oṁ kalādhārāyai svāhā
She who supports all talents

- 117 -

ॐ कालदैत्यनिकृन्तिन्यै स्वाहा

oṁ kāladaityanikṛntinyai svāhā
She who makes the time of duality

- 118 -

ॐ कामिन्यै स्वाहा

oṁ kāminyai svāhā
She who is desired

- 119 -

ॐ कामवन्द्यायै स्वाहा

oṁ kāmavandyāyai svāhā
She who is the most highly praised desire

- 120 -

ॐ कमनीयायै स्वाहा

oṁ kamanīyāyai svāhā
She who is the object of desire

- 121 -

ॐ विनोदिन्यै स्वाहा

oṁ vinodinyai svāhā
She who is playful

- 122 -

ॐ कामसुवे स्वाहा

oṁ kāmasuve svāhā
She who is a desire

- 123 -

ॐ कामवनितायै स्वाहा

oṁ kāmavanitāyai svāhā
She who is the desire that is most beloved

- 124 -

ॐ कामधुरे स्वाहा

oṁ kāmadhure svāhā
She who is the desire that is difficult to attain

- 125 -

ॐ कमलावत्यै स्वाहा

oṁ kamalāvatyai svāhā
She who is the spirit of the one who sits on a Lotus

- 126 -

ॐ कामायै स्वाहा

oṁ kāmāyai svāhā
She who is all desires

- 127 -

ॐ कराल्यै स्वाहा

oṁ karālyai svāhā
She who is terrifying

- 128 -

ॐ कामकेलिविनोदिन्यै स्वाहा

oṁ kāmakelivinodinyai svāhā
She who is greatly desired

- 129 -

ॐ कामनायै स्वाहा

oṁ kāmanāyai svāhā
She who leads desire

- 130 -

ॐ कामदायै स्वाहा

oṁ kāmadāyai svāhā
She who gives desire

- 131 -

ॐ काम्यायै स्वाहा

oṁ kāmyāyai svāhā
She who is desire

- 132 -

ॐ कमलायै स्वाहा

oṁ kamalāyai svāhā
She who is a lotus

- 133 -

ॐ कमलार्चितायै स्वाहा

oṁ kamalārcitāyai svāhā
She who is offered a lotus

- 134 -

ॐ काश्मीरलिप्तवक्षोजायै स्वाहा

oṁ kāśmīraliptavakṣojāyai svāhā
She whose breast is smeared with red unguents

- 135 -

ॐ काश्मीरद्रवचर्चितायै स्वाहा

oṁ kāśmīradravacarcitāyai svāhā
She who is offered red articles

- 136 -

ॐ कनकायै स्वाहा

oṁ kanakāyai svāhā
She who is gold

- 137 -

ॐ कनकप्राणायै स्वाहा

oṁ kanakaprāṇāyai svāhā
She who is the life force of gold

- 138 -

ॐ कनकाचलवासिन्यै स्वाहा

oṁ kanakācalavāsinyai svāhā

She who resides upon the golden mountain

- 139 -

ॐ कनकाभायै स्वाहा

oṁ kanakābhāyai svāhā

She who is the shine of gold

- 140 -

ॐ काननस्थायै स्वाहा

oṁ kānanasthāyai svāhā

She who dwells in the ears

- 141 -

ॐ कामाख्यायै स्वाहा

oṁ kāmākhyāyai svāhā

She who is the seer of desire

- 142 -

ॐ कनकप्रदायै स्वाहा

oṁ kanakapradāyai svāhā

She who bestows gold

- 143 -

ॐ कामपीठस्थितायै स्वाहा

oṁ kāmapīṭhasthitāyai svāhā

She who is situated in the pilgrimage place of desire

- 144 -

ॐ नित्यायै स्वाहा

oṁ nityāyai svāhā
She who is eternal

- 145 -

ॐ कामधामनिवासिन्यै स्वाहा

oṁ kāmadhāmanivāsinyai svāhā
She who resides in the holy place of desire

- 146 -

ॐ कंबुकण्ठ्यै स्वाहा

oṁ kaṁbukaṇṭhyai svāhā
She who has wrinkles on her neck

- 147 -

ॐ करालाक्ष्यै स्वाहा

oṁ karālākṣyai svāhā
She who has formidable eyes

- 148 -

ॐ किशोर्यै स्वाहा

oṁ kiśoryai svāhā
She who is youthful

- 149 -

ॐ चलानादिन्यै स्वाहा

oṁ calānādinyai svāhā
She who has the vibrations of movement

- 150 -

ॐ कलायै स्वाहा

oṁ kalāyai svāhā
She who has art

- 151 -

ॐ काष्ठायै स्वाहा

oṁ kāṣṭhāyai svāhā
She who is the highest limit

- 152 -

ॐ निमेषायै स्वाहा

oṁ nimeṣāyai svāhā
She who is goddess of the moment

- 153 -

ॐ कालस्थायै स्वाहा

oṁ kālasthāyai svāhā
She who resides in time

- 154 -

ॐ कालरूपिण्यै स्वाहा

oṁ kālarūpiṇyai svāhā
She who is the form of time

- 155 -

ॐ कालज्ञायै स्वाहा

oṁ kālajñāyai svāhā
She who is the knowledge of time

- 156 -

ॐ कालमात्रायै स्वाहा

oṁ kālamātrāyai svāhā
She who is the mother of time

- 157 -

ॐ कालधात्र्यै स्वाहा

oṁ kāladhātryai svāhā
She who is the creator of time

- 158 -

ॐ कलावत्यै स्वाहा

oṁ kalāvatyai svāhā
She who is the spirit of the arts

- 159 -

ॐ कालदायै स्वाहा

oṁ kāladāyai svāhā
She who is the giver of time

- 160 -

ॐ कालहायै स्वाहा

oṁ kālahāyai svāhā
She who is the destroyer of time

- 161 -

ॐ कुल्यायै स्वाहा

oṁ kulyāyai svāhā
She who is with the multitudes

\- 162 -

ॐ कुरकुल्लायै स्वाहा

oṁ kurakullāyai svāhā

She who is with the multitudes who perform actions

\- 163 -

ॐ कुलाङ्गनायै स्वाहा

oṁ kulāṅganāyai svāhā

She who is with the individuals in the community

\- 164 -

ॐ कीर्तिदायै स्वाहा

oṁ kīrtidāyai svāhā

She who is the giver of fame

\- 165 -

ॐ कीर्तिहायै स्वाहा

oṁ kīrtihāyai svāhā

She who is the destroyer of fame

\- 166 -

ॐ कीर्त्यै स्वाहा

oṁ kīrtyai svāhā

She who is fame

\- 167 -

ॐ कीर्तिस्थायै स्वाहा

oṁ kīrtisthāyai svāhā

She who resides in fame

- 168 -

ॐ कीर्त्तिवर्धिन्यै स्वाहा

oṁ kīrttivardhinyai svāhā
She who apportions fame

- 169 -

ॐ कीर्त्तिज्ञायै स्वाहा

oṁ kīrttijñāyai svāhā
She who knows fame

- 170 -

ॐ कीर्त्तिपदायै स्वाहा

oṁ kīrttipadāyai svāhā
She who gives the austerity of fame

- 171 -

ॐ कृत्तिकायै स्वाहा

oṁ kṛttikāyai svāhā
She who is the cause of fame

- 172 -

ॐ केशवप्रियायै स्वाहा

oṁ keśavapriyāyai svāhā
She who is the beloved of Keśava (Kṛṣṇa)

- 173 -

ॐ केशिहायै स्वाहा

oṁ keśihāyai svāhā
She who takes away the hair

- 174 -

ॐ केलिकायै स्वाहा

oṁ kelikāyai svāhā
She who engages in amorous sports

- 175 -

ॐ केशवानन्दकारिण्यै स्वाहा

oṁ keśavānandakāriṇyai svāhā
She who is the cause of bliss to Keśava

- 176 -

ॐ कुमुदाभायै स्वाहा

oṁ kumudābhāyai svāhā
She who is the lustre of the moon

- 177 -

ॐ कुमार्यै स्वाहा

oṁ kumāryai svāhā
She who is the ever pure one

- 178 -

ॐ कर्मदायै स्वाहा

oṁ karmadāyai svāhā
She who is the giver of action

- 179 -

ॐ कमलेक्षणायै स्वाहा

oṁ kamalekṣaṇāyai svāhā
She who has lotus eyes

- 180 -

ॐ कौमुद्यै स्वाहा

oṁ kaumudyai svāhā
She who is the cause of the full moon

- 181 -

ॐ कुमुदानन्दायै स्वाहा

oṁ kumudānandāyai svāhā
She who is the bliss of the full moon

- 182 -

ॐ कालिक्यै स्वाहा

oṁ kālikyai svāhā
She who is beyond time

- 183 -

ॐ कुमुद्वत्यै स्वाहा

oṁ kumudvatyai svāhā
She who is the spirit of the moon

- 184 -

ॐ कोदण्डधारिण्यै स्वाहा

oṁ kodaṇḍadhāriṇyai svāhā
She who supports punishment

- 185 -

ॐ क्रोधायै स्वाहा

oṁ krodhāyai svāhā
She who is angry

- 186 -

ॐ कूटस्थायै स्वाहा

oṁ kūṭasthāyai svāhā

She who resides at the summit

- 187 -

ॐ कोटराश्रयायै स्वाहा

oṁ koṭarāśrayāyai svāhā

She who takes refuge in excellence

- 188 -

ॐ कलकण्ठ्यै स्वाहा

oṁ kalakaṇṭhyai svāhā

She who has a dark throat

- 189 -

ॐ करलाङ्ग्यै स्वाहा

oṁ karalāṅgyai svāhā

She who has a terrifying body

- 190 -

ॐ कालाङ्ग्यै स्वाहा

oṁ kālāṅgyai svāhā

She who is the limbs of time

- 191 -

ॐ कालभूषणायै स्वाहा

oṁ kālabhūṣaṇāyai svāhā

She who is the illumination of time

- 192 -

ॐ कंकाल्यै स्वाहा

oṁ kaṁkālyai svāhā
She who has a skull in her hand

- 193 -

ॐ कामदामायै स्वाहा

oṁ kāmadāmāyai svāhā
She who makes desires to be at peace

- 194 -

ॐ कङ्कालकृतभूषणायै स्वाहा

oṁ kaṅkālakṛtabhūṣaṇāyai svāhā
She who creates skulls as an ornament

- 195 -

ॐ कपालकर्तृककरायै स्वाहा

oṁ kapālakartṛkakarāyai svāhā
She who is the cause of the creation of skulls

- 196 -

ॐ करवीरस्वरूपिण्यै स्वाहा

oṁ karavīrasvarūpiṇyai svāhā
She who is the intrinsic nature of the hero of action

- 197 -

ॐ कपर्दिन्यै स्वाहा

oṁ kapardinyai svāhā
She who wears knotted hair

- 198 -

ॐ कोमलाङ्ग्यै स्वाहा

oṁ komalāṅgyai svāhā

She whose limbs are soft and tender

- 199 -

ॐ कृपासिन्धवे स्वाहा

oṁ kṛpāsindhave svāhā

She who is the ocean of grace

- 200 -

ॐ कृपामय्यै स्वाहा

oṁ kṛpāmayyai svāhā

She who is the manifestation of grace

- 201 -

ॐ कुशावत्यै स्वाहा

oṁ kuśāvatyai svāhā

She who is the spirit of purifying light

- 202 -

ॐ कुण्डसंस्थायै स्वाहा

oṁ kuṇḍasaṁsthāyai svāhā

She who is situated in a container

- 203 -

ॐ कौवेर्यै स्वाहा

oṁ kauveryai svāhā

She who is full of wealth

- 204 -

ॐ कौशिक्यै स्वाहा

oṁ kauśikyai svāhā
She who comes from within

- 205 -

ॐ काश्यप्यै स्वाहा

oṁ kāśyapyai svāhā
She who shines like the sun

- 206 -

ॐ कद्रूतनयायै स्वाहा

oṁ kadrutanayāyai svāhā
She who embodies the mother of earthly beings

- 207 -

ॐ कलिकल्मषनाशिन्यै स्वाहा

oṁ kalikalmaṣanāśinyai svāhā
She who destroys the darkness of Kali Yuga

- 208 -

ॐ कञ्जज्ञायै स्वाहा

oṁ kañjajñāyai svāhā
She who knows the lotus

- 209 -

ॐ कञ्जवदनायै स्वाहा

oṁ kañjavadanāyai svāhā
She whose face is like a lotus

\- 210 -

ॐ कञ्जकिञ्जल्कचर्चितायै स्वाहा

oṁ kañjakiñjalkacarcitāyai svāhā
She who is offered lotuses

\- 211 -

ॐ कञ्जाभायै स्वाहा

oṁ kañjābhāyai svāhā
She who shines like a lotus

\- 212 -

ॐ कञ्जमध्यस्थायै स्वाहा

oṁ kañjamadhyasthāyai svāhā
She who is situated in the middle of a lotus

\- 213 -

ॐ कञ्जनेत्रायै स्वाहा

oṁ kañjanetrāyai svāhā
She who has lotus eyes

\- 214 -

ॐ कचोद्भवायै स्वाहा

oṁ kacodbhavāyai svāhā
She who has a being like a tortoise

\- 215 -

ॐ कामरूपायै स्वाहा

oṁ kāmarūpāyai svāhā
She who is the form of desire

- 216 -

ॐ ह्रींकार्यै स्वाहा

oṁ hrīṁkāryai svāhā
She who is the letter Hriṁ

- 217 -

ॐ कश्यपान्वयवर्धिन्यै स्वाहा

oṁ kaśyapānvayavardhinyai svāhā
She who distributes light like the sun

- 218 -

ॐ खर्वायै स्वाहा

oṁ kharvāyai svāhā
She who is imperfect

- 219 -

ॐ खञ्जनद्वन्द्वलोचनायै स्वाहा

oṁ khañjanadvandvalocanāyai svāhā
She who has the darting eyes of a small bird

- 220 -

ॐ खर्ववाहिन्यै स्वाहा

oṁ kharvavāhinyai svāhā
She who carries the crippled

- 221 -

ॐ खङ्गिन्यै स्वाहा

oṁ khaṅginyai svāhā
She who wields the sword of wisdom

\- 222 -

ॐ खड्गहस्तायै स्वाहा

oṁ khaṅgahastāyai svāhā
She who has the sword of wisdom in her hand

\- 223 -

ॐ खेचर्यै स्वाहा

oṁ khecaryai svāhā
She who flys through space

\- 224 -

ॐ खड्गरूपिण्यै स्वाहा

oṁ khaṅgarūpiṇyai svāhā
She who has the intrinsic nature of the sword of wisdom

\- 225 -

ॐ खगस्थायै स्वाहा

oṁ khagasthāyai svāhā
She who is situated in the the sword of wisdom

\- 226 -

ॐ खगरूपायै स्वाहा

oṁ khagarūpāyai svāhā
She who is the form of the sword of wisdom

\- 227 -

ॐ खगगायै स्वाहा

oṁ khagagāyai svāhā
She who moves with the sword of wisdom

- 228 -

ॐ खगसम्भवायै स्वाहा

oṁ khagasambhavāyai svāhā

She who exists with the sword of wisdom

- 229 -

ॐ खगधात्र्यै स्वाहा

oṁ khagadhātryai svāhā

She who is creator of the sword of wisdom

- 230 -

ॐ खगानन्दायै स्वाहा

oṁ khagānandāyai svāhā

She who is the bliss of the sword of wisdom

- 231 -

ॐ खगयोनिस्वरूपिण्यै स्वाहा

oṁ khagayonisvarūpiṇyai svāhā

She who is the intrinsic nature of the womb of the sword of wisdom

- 232 -

ॐ खगेश्यै स्वाहा

oṁ khageśyai svāhā

She who is the seer of the sword of wisdom

- 233 -

ॐ खेटककरायै स्वाहा

oṁ kheṭakakarāyai svāhā

She who causes the activities of the farmers

\- 234 -

ॐ खगानन्दविवर्धिन्यै स्वाहा

oṁ khagānandavivardhinyai svāhā

She who ditributes the bliss of the sword of wisdom

\- 235 -

ॐ खगमान्यायै स्वाहा

oṁ khagamānyāyai svāhā

She who obeys the sword of wisdom

\- 236 -

ॐ खगाधारायै स्वाहा

oṁ khagādhārāyai svāhā

She who supports the sword of wisdom

\- 237 -

ॐ खगगर्वविमोचिन्यै स्वाहा

oṁ khagagarvavimocinyai svāhā

She who annihilates the pride in the sword of wisdom

\- 238 -

ॐ गङ्गायै स्वाहा

oṁ gaṅgāyai svāhā

She who is the Ganges

\- 239 -

ॐ गोदावर्यै स्वाहा

oṁ godāvaryai svāhā

She who is Godāvari

- 240 -

ॐ गीत्यै स्वाहा

oṁ gītyai svāhā
She who is song

- 241 -

ॐ गायत्र्यै स्वाहा

oṁ gāyatryai svāhā
She who is Gāyatri

- 242 -

ॐ गगनाल्यायै स्वाहा

oṁ gaganālayāyai svāhā
She who resides with the wind

- 243 -

ॐ गीर्वाणसुन्दर्यै स्वाहा

oṁ gīrvāṇsundaryai svāhā
She who is beautiful poetry

- 244 -

ॐ गवे स्वाहा

oṁ gave svāhā
She who is with cows

- 245 -

ॐ गाधायै स्वाहा

oṁ gādhāyai svāhā
She who stands firmly

- 246 -

ॐ गीर्वाणपूजितायै स्वाहा

oṁ gīrvāṇapūjitāyai svāhā
She who is worshipped with poetry

- 247 -

ॐ गीर्वाणचर्चितपदायै स्वाहा

oṁ gīrvāṇcarcitapadāyai svāhā
She who is offered poetry

- 248 -

ॐ गान्धार्यै स्वाहा

oṁ gāndhāryai svāhā
She who is from the land of music

- 249 -

ॐ गोमत्यै स्वाहा

oṁ gomatyai svāhā
She who is the mother of light

- 250-

ॐ गर्विण्यै स्वाहा

oṁ garviṇyai svāhā
She who is proud

- 251 -

ॐ गर्वहन्त्र्यै स्वाहा

oṁ garvahantryai svāhā
She who destroys pride

- 252 -

ॐ गर्भस्थायै स्वाहा

oṁ garbhasthāyai svāhā
She who is situated in the womb

- 253 -

ॐ गर्भधारिण्यै स्वाहा

oṁ garbhadhāriṇyai svāhā
She who supports the womb

- 254 -

ॐ गर्भदायै स्वाहा

oṁ garbhadāyai svāhā
She who gives the womb

- 255 -

ॐ गर्भहन्त्र्यै स्वाहा

oṁ garbhahantryai svāhā
She who takes away the womb

- 256 -

ॐ गन्धर्वकुलपूजितायै स्वाहा

oṁ gandharvakulapūjitāyai svāhā
She who is worshipped by the family of Gandharvas

- 257 -

ॐ गयायै स्वाहा

oṁ gayāyai svāhā
She who is wisdom

- 258 -

ॐ गौर्यै स्वाहा

oṁ gauryai svāhā
She who is rays of light

- 259 -

ॐ गिरिराजायै स्वाहा

oṁ girirājāyai svāhā
She who dwells in the kingdom of mountains

- 260 -

ॐ गिरिस्थायै स्वाहा

oṁ giristhāyai svāhā
She who resides in the mountains

- 261 -

ॐ गिरिसम्भवायै स्वाहा

oṁ girisambhavāyai svāhā
She who exists in mountains

- 262 -

ॐ गिरिगह्वरमध्यस्थायै स्वाहा

oṁ girigahvaramadhyasthāyai svāhā
She who is situated in the midst of the mountains

- 263 -

ॐ कुञ्जरेश्वरगामिन्यै स्वाहा

oṁ kuñjareśvaragāminyai svāhā
She who moves with the lord of wealth

- 264 -

ॐ किरीटिन्यै स्वाहा

oṁ kirīṭinyai svāhā
She who is decorated with a crown

- 265 -

ॐ गदिन्यै स्वाहा

oṁ gadinyai svāhā
She who sits on the seat

- 266 -

ॐ गुञ्जाहारविभूषणायै स्वाहा

oṁ guñjāhāravibhūṣaṇāyai svāhā
She who shines with a priceless necklace

- 267 -

ॐ गणपायै स्वाहा

oṁ gaṇapāyai svāhā
She who is the protector of the multitudes

- 268 -

ॐ गणकायै स्वाहा

oṁ gaṇakāyai svāhā
She who is the cause of the multitudes

- 269 -

ॐ गुण्यायै स्वाहा

oṁ guṇyāyai svāhā
She who has qualities

\- 270 -

ॐ गुणकानन्दकारिण्यै स्वाहा

oṁ guṇakānandakāriṇyai svāhā

She who is the cause of all blissful qualities

\- 271 -

ॐ गुणपूज्यायै स्वाहा

oṁ guṇapūjyāyai svāhā

She whose qualities are worshipped

\- 272 -

ॐ गीर्वाणायै स्वाहा

oṁ gīrvāṇāyai svāhā

She whose words are like the song

\- 273 -

ॐ गणपानन्दविवर्धिन्यै स्वाहा

oṁ gaṇapānandavivardhinyai svāhā

She who distributes the bliss to the multitudes

\- 274 -

ॐ गुरुरमात्रायै स्वाहा

oṁ gururamātrāyai svāhā

She who is the mother of gurus

\- 275 -

ॐ गुरुरतायै स्वाहा

oṁ gururatāyai svāhā

She who is the support of gurus

- 276 -

ॐ गुरुभक्तिपरायणायै स्वाहा

oṁ gurubhaktiparāyaṇāyai svāhā
She who always has devotion to gurus

- 277 -

ॐ गोत्रायै स्वाहा

oṁ gotrāyai svāhā
She who is the lineage of wisdom

- 278 -

ॐ गवे स्वाहा

oṁ gave svāhā
She who pours forth goodness

- 279 -

ॐ कृष्णभगिन्यै स्वाहा

oṁ kṛṣṇabhaginyai svāhā
She who is the partner of the doer of all

- 280 -

ॐ कृष्णसुवे स्वाहा

oṁ kṛṣṇasuve svāhā
She who is the excellence of the doer of all

- 281 -

ॐ कृष्णनन्दिन्यै स्वाहा

oṁ kṛṣṇanandinyai svāhā
She who gives birth to the bliss of the doer of all

- 282 -

ॐ गोवर्धन्यै स्वाहा

oṁ govardhanyai svāhā
She who raises the Govardhana Mountain

- 283 -

ॐ गोत्रधरायै स्वाहा

oṁ gotradharāyai svāhā
She who supports the lineage of wisdom

- 284 -

ॐ गोवर्धनकृतालयायै स्वाहा

oṁ govardhanakṛtālayāyai svāhā
She who creates and destroys the Govardhana Mountain

- 285 -

ॐ गोवर्धनधरायै स्वाहा

oṁ govardhanadharāyai svāhā
She who supports the Govardhana Mountain

- 286 -

ॐ गोदायै स्वाहा

oṁ godāyai svāhā
She who gives light

- 287 -

ॐ गौराङ्ग्यै स्वाहा

oṁ gaurāṅgyai svāhā
She whose limbs emanate lights

- 288 -

ॐ गौतमात्मजायै स्वाहा

oṁ gautamātmajāyai svāhā
She who gives birth to the soul of Gautam

- 289 -

ॐ घर्घरायै स्वाहा

oṁ ghargharāyai svāhā
She who shouts

- 290 -

ॐ घोररूपायै स्वाहा

oṁ ghorarūpāyai svāhā
She who is the form of a horse

- 291 -

ॐ घोरायै स्वाहा

oṁ ghorāyai svāhā
She who rides a horse

- 292 -

ॐ घर्घरनादिन्यै स्वाहा

oṁ ghargharanādinyai svāhā
She who shouts with a loud voice

- 293 -

ॐ श्यामायै स्वाहा

oṁ śyāmāyai svāhā
She who is dark

- 294 -

ॐ घनरवायै स्वाहा

oṁ ghanaravāyai svāhā
She who roars like a cloud

- 295 -

ॐ अघोरायै स्वाहा

oṁ aghorāyai svāhā
She who is fearless

- 296 -

ॐ घनायै स्वाहा

oṁ ghanāyai svāhā
She who is uninterrupted auspiciousness

- 297 -

ॐ घोरार्त्तिनाशिन्यै स्वाहा

oṁ ghorārttināśinyai svāhā
She who destroys frightful enemies

- 298 -

ॐ घनस्थायै स्वाहा

oṁ ghanasthāyai svāhā
She who resides in uninterrupted auspiciousness

- 299 -

ॐ घनानन्दायै स्वाहा

oṁ ghanānandāyai svāhā
She who is the bliss of uninterrupted auspiciousness

- 300 -

ॐ दारिद्र्यघननाशिन्यै स्वाहा

oṁ dāridryaghananāśinyai svāhā
She who destroys affliction

- 301 -

ॐ चित्तज्ञायै स्वाहा

oṁ cittajñāyai svāhā
She who knows consciousness

- 302 -

ॐ चिन्तितपदायै स्वाहा

oṁ cintitapadāyai svāhā
She who gives anxiety

- 303 -

ॐ चित्तस्थायै स्वाहा

oṁ cittasthāyai svāhā
She who resides in all thought and recollection

- 304 -

ॐ चित्तरूपिण्यै स्वाहा

oṁ cittarūpiṇyai svāhā
She who is the intrinsic nature of all thought and recollection

- 305 -

ॐ चक्रिण्यै स्वाहा

oṁ cakriṇyai svāhā
She who holds the discus

- 306 -

ॐ चारुचम्पाभायै स्वाहा

oṁ cārucampābhāyai svāhā
She who shines in the darkness

- 307 -

ॐ चारुचम्पकमालिन्यै स्वाहा

oṁ cārucampakamālinyai svāhā
She who wears a garland of dark flowers

- 308 -

ॐ चन्द्रिकायै स्वाहा

oṁ candrikāyai svāhā
She who tears apart the duality of thought

- 309 -

ॐ चन्द्रकान्त्यै स्वाहा

oṁ candrakāntyai svāhā
She who is the beauty of the moon

- 310 -

ॐ चाषिन्यै स्वाहा

oṁ cāṣinyai svāhā
She who is a blue jay

- 311 -

ॐ चन्द्रशेखरायै स्वाहा

oṁ candraśekharāyai svāhā
She who wears the moon on her crown

- 312 -

ॐ चण्डिकायै स्वाहा

oṁ caṇḍikāyai svāhā
She who tears apart thought

- 313 -

ॐ चण्डदैत्यघन्यै स्वाहा

oṁ caṇḍadaityaghanyai svāhā
She who destroys the duality of passion

- 314 -

ॐ चन्द्रशेखरवल्लभायै स्वाहा

oṁ candraśekharavallabhāyai svāhā
She who is the strength of he who wears the moon

- 315 -

ॐ चाण्डालिन्यै स्वाहा

oṁ cāṇḍālinyai svāhā
She who is outcast

- 316 -

ॐ चामुण्डायै स्वाहा

oṁ cāmuṇḍāyai svāhā
She who slayed anger and passion

- 317 -

ॐ चण्डमुण्डवधोद्यतायै स्वाहा

oṁ caṇḍamuṇḍavadhodyatāyai svāhā
She who rose after slaying anger and passion

- 318 -

ॐ चैतन्यभैरव्यै स्वाहा

oṁ caitanyabhairavyai svāhā
She who is the fearful consciousness

- 319 -

ॐ चण्डायै स्वाहा

oṁ caṇḍāyai svāhā
She who is passionate

- 320 -

ॐ चैतन्यघनगेहिन्यै स्वाहा

oṁ caitanyaghanagehinyai svāhā
She who moves with the uninterrupted auspiciousness of consciousness

- 321 -

ॐ चित्स्वरूपायै स्वाहा

oṁ citsvarūpāyai svāhā
She who is the form of consciousness

- 322 -

ॐ चिदाधारायै स्वाहा

oṁ cidādhārāyai svāhā
She who supports consciousness

- 323 -

ॐ चण्डवेगायै स्वाहा

oṁ caṇḍavegāyai svāhā
She who destroys anger

- 324 -

ॐ चिदालयायै स्वाहा

oṁ cidālayāyai svāhā

She who dissolves into consciousness

- 325 -

ॐ चन्द्रमण्डलमध्यस्थायै स्वाहा

oṁ candramaṇḍalamadhyasthāyai svāhā

She who resides in the middle of the realm of the moon

- 326 -

ॐ चन्द्रकोटिसुशीलतायै स्वाहा

oṁ candrakoṭisuśīlatāyai svāhā

She who is as cool as ten million moons

- 327 -

ॐ चपलायै स्वाहा

oṁ capalāyai svāhā

She who is inconstant

- 328 -

ॐ चन्द्रभगिन्यै स्वाहा

oṁ candrabhaginyai svāhā

She who is the partner of the moon

- 329 -

ॐ चन्द्रकोटिनिभाननायै स्वाहा

oṁ candrakoṭinibhānanāyai svāhā

She who shines like ten million moons

- 330 -

ॐ चिन्तामणिगुणाधारायै स्वाहा

oṁ cintāmaṇiguṇādhārāyai svāhā

She who supports the jewel-like qualities of thought

- 331 -

ॐ चिन्तामणिविभूषणायै स्वाहा

oṁ cintāmaṇivibhūṣaṇāyai svāhā

She whose thoughts shine like gems

- 332 -

ॐ चित्तचिन्तामणिकृतालयायै स्वाहा

oṁ cittacintāmaṇikṛtālayāyai svāhā

She who creates and destroys the jewels of thought and recollection

- 333 -

ॐ चिन्तामणिकृतालयायै स्वाहा

oṁ cintāmaṇikṛtālayāyai svāhā

She who creates and destroys the jewels of thought

- 334 -

ॐ चारुचन्दनलिप्ताङ्ग्यै स्वाहा

oṁ cārucandanaliptāṅgyai svāhā

She who has pleasing sandal paste annointing her body

- 335 -

ॐ चतुरायै स्वाहा

oṁ caturāyai svāhā

She who is the four

- 336 -

ॐ चतुर्मुख्यै स्वाहा

oṁ caturmukhyai svāhā
She who has four faces

- 337 -

ॐ चैतन्यदायै स्वाहा

oṁ caitanyadāyai svāhā
She who gives consciousness

- 338 -

ॐ चिदानन्दायै स्वाहा

oṁ cidānandāyai svāhā
She who gives the bliss of consciousness

- 339 -

ॐ चारुचामरवीजितायै स्वाहा

oṁ cārucāmaravījitāyai svāhā
She who is delightfully fanned by a yak's tail

- 340 -

ॐ छत्रदायै स्वाहा

oṁ chatradāyai svāhā
She who gives refuge

- 341 -

ॐ छत्रधार्यै स्वाहा

oṁ chatradhāryai svāhā
She who supports the refuge

- 342 -

ॐ छलच्छद्मविनाशिन्यै स्वाहा

oṁ chalachadmavināśinyai svāhā
She who destroys deceit

- 343 -

ॐ छत्रहायै स्वाहा

oṁ chatrahāyai svāhā
She who takes away the refuge

- 344 -

ॐ छत्ररूपायै स्वाहा

oṁ chatrarūpāyai svāhā
She who is the form of refuge

- 345 -

ॐ छत्रच्छायाकृतालयायै स्वाहा

oṁ chatrachāyākṛtālayāyai svāhā
She who creates and destroys the reflection of refuge

- 346 -

ॐ जगजीवायै स्वाहा

oṁ jagajīvāyai svāhā
She who is perceived as life

- 347 -

ॐ जगद्धात्र्यै स्वाहा

oṁ jagaddhātryai svāhā
She who creates perceivable existence

- 348 -

ॐ जगदानन्दकारिण्यै स्वाहा

oṁ jagadānandakāriṇyai svāhā
She who is the cause of the bliss of perceivable existence

-349 -

ॐ यज्ञप्रियायै स्वाहा

oṁ yajñapriyāyai svāhā
She who loves sacrifice

- 350 -

ॐ यज्ञरतायै स्वाहा

oṁ yajñaratāyai svāhā
She who appreciates sacrifice

- 351 -

ॐ जपयज्ञपरायणायै स्वाहा

oṁ japayajñaparāyaṇāyai svāhā
She who always performs the sacrifice of japa

- 352 -

ॐ जनन्यै स्वाहा

oṁ jananyai svāhā
She who is the mother

- 353 -

ॐ जानक्यै स्वाहा

oṁ jānakyai svāhā
She who is the father

- 354 -

ॐ यज्वायै स्वाहा

oṁ yajvāyai svāhā
She who shines with sacrifice

- 355 -

ॐ यज्ञहायै स्वाहा

oṁ yajñahāyai svāhā
She who takes away the sacrifice

- 356 -

ॐ यज्ञनन्दिन्यै स्वाहा

oṁ yajñanandinyai svāhā
She who is the delight of sacrifice

- 357 -

ॐ यज्ञदायै स्वाहा

oṁ yajñadāyai svāhā
She who gives sacrifice

- 358 -

ॐ यज्ञफलदायै स्वाहा

oṁ yajñaphaladāyai svāhā
She who gives the fruit of sacrifice

- 359 -

ॐ यज्ञस्थानकृतालयायै स्वाहा

oṁ yajñasthānakṛtālayāyai svāhā
She who creates and destroys the place of sacrifice

- 360 -

ॐ यज्ञभोक्त्यै स्वाहा

oṁ yajñabhoktyai svāhā
She who enjoys sacrifice

- 361 -

ॐ यज्ञरूपायै स्वाहा

oṁ yajñarūpāyai svāhā
She who is the form of sacrifice

- 362 -

ॐ यज्ञविघ्नविनाशिन्यै स्वाहा

oṁ yajñvighnavināśinyai svāhā
She who destroys the obstacles to sacrifice

- 363 -

ॐ जपाकुसुमसङ्काशायै स्वाहा

oṁ japākusumasaṅkāśāyai svāhā
She who is the delightfully fragrant hibiscus flower

- 364 -

ॐ जपाकुसुमशोभितायै स्वाहा

oṁ japākusumaśobhitāyai svāhā
She who is the shine of the fragrant hibiscus flower

- 365 -

ॐ जालंधर्यै स्वाहा

oṁ jālaṁdharyai svāhā
She whose being is magical

- 366 -

ॐ जयायै स्वाहा

oṁ jayāyai svāhā
She who gives birth

- 367 -

ॐ जैत्र्यै स्वाहा

oṁ jaitryai svāhā
She who bears the three

- 368 -

ॐ जीमुतचयभाषिण्यै स्वाहा

oṁ jīmutacayabhāṣiṇyai svāhā
She who shines with the rays of the sun

- 369 -

ॐ जयदायै स्वाहा

oṁ jayadāyai svāhā
She who gives victory

- 370 -

ॐ जयरूपायै स्वाहा

oṁ jayarūpāyai svāhā
She who is the form of victory

- 371 -

ॐ जयस्थायै स्वाहा

oṁ jayasthāyai svāhā
She who resides in victory

- 372 -

ॐ जयकारिण्यै स्वाहा

oṁ jayakāriṇyai svāhā
She who is the cause of victory

- 373 -

ॐ जगदीशप्रियायै स्वाहा

oṁ jagadīśapriyāyai svāhā
She who is the beloved ruler of perceivable existence

- 374 -

ॐ जीवायै स्वाहा

oṁ jīvāyai svāhā
She who is life

- 375 -

ॐ जलस्थायै स्वाहा

oṁ jalasthāyai svāhā
She who resides in water

- 376 -

ॐ जलजेक्षनायै स्वाहा

oṁ jalajekṣanāyai svāhā
She who is water in the lotus-eyes

- 377 -

ॐ जलरूपायै स्वाहा

oṁ jalarūpāyai svāhā
She who is the form of water

- 378 -

ॐ जह्नुकन्यायै स्वाहा

oṁ jahnukanyāyai svāhā
She who is the daughter of the Ganges

- 379 -

ॐ यमुनायै स्वाहा

oṁ yamunāyai svāhā
She who is the Yamuna

- 380 -

ॐ जलजोदर्यै स्वाहा

oṁ jalajodaryai svāhā
She whose waist is [slender] like a lotus

- 381 -

ॐ जलजास्यायै स्वाहा

oṁ jalajāsyāyai svāhā
She whose face is [beautiful] like a lotus

- 382 -

ॐ जाह्नव्यै स्वाहा

oṁ jāhnavyai svāhā
She who is the Ganges

- 383 -

ॐ जलजाभायै स्वाहा

oṁ jalajābhāyai svāhā
She who gives birth to shining waters

- 384 -

ॐ जलोदर्यै स्वाहा

oṁ jalodaryai svāhā
She who is the rising waters

- 385 -

ॐ यदुवंशीद्भवायै स्वाहा

oṁ yaduvaṁśīdbhavāyai svāhā
She who exists in the family of Yadu (Kṛṣṇa)

- 386 -

ॐ जीवायै स्वाहा

oṁ jīvāyai svāhā
She who is the tongue

- 387 -

ॐ यादवानन्दकारिण्यै स्वाहा

oṁ yādavānanandakāriṇyai svāhā
She who is the cause of bliss to the Yadavs (cow herders)

- 388 -

ॐ यशोदायै स्वाहा

oṁ yaśodāyai svāhā
She who is Yaśoda (the mother of Kṛṣṇa)

- 389 -

ॐ यशसांराश्यै स्वाहा

oṁ yaśasāṁrāśyai svāhā
She who expands fame

- 390 -

ॐ यशोदानन्दकारिण्यै स्वाहा

oṁ yaśodānandakāriṇyai svāhā
She who is the cause of bliss to Yaśoda

- 391 -

ॐ ज्वलिन्यै स्वाहा

oṁ jvalinyai svāhā
She who shines

- 392 -

ॐ ज्वालिन्यै स्वाहा

oṁ jvālinyai svāhā
She who causes others to shine

- 393 -

ॐ ज्वालायै स्वाहा

oṁ jvālāyai svāhā
She who is radiance

- 394 -

ॐ ज्वलत्पावकसन्निभायै स्वाहा

oṁ jvalatpāvakasannibhāyai svāhā
She whose light shines

- 395 -

ॐ ज्वालामुख्यै स्वाहा

oṁ jvālāmukhyai svāhā
She whose face shines

- 396 -

ॐ जगन्मात्रे स्वाहा

oṁ jaganmātre svāhā
She who is the mother of the perceivable universe

- 397 -

ॐ यमलार्जुनभञ्जकायै स्वाहा

oṁ yamalārjunabhañjakāyai svāhā
She who uproots adversity

- 398 -

ॐ जन्मदायै स्वाहा

oṁ janmadāyai svāhā
She who gives birth

- 399 -

ॐ जन्मह्यै स्वाहा

oṁ janmahyai svāhā
She who takes birth

- 400 -

ॐ जन्यायै स्वाहा

oṁ janyāyai svāhā
She who is born

- 401 -

ॐ जन्मभुवे स्वाहा

oṁ janmabhuve svāhā
She who gives birth to existence

- 402 -

ॐ जनकात्मजायै स्वाहा

oṁ janakātmajāyai svāhā
She who gives birth to the soul of the father

- 403 -

ॐ जनानन्दायै स्वाहा

oṁ janānandāyai svāhā
She who gives bliss to the people

- 404 -

ॐ जाम्बवत्यै स्वाहा

oṁ jāmbavatyai svāhā
She who is wisest of the monkeys

- 405 -

ॐ जम्बूद्वीपकृतालयायै स्वाहा

oṁ jambūdvīpakṛtālayāyai svāhā
She who creates and destroys the islands of being

- 406 -

ॐ जाम्बूनदसमानाभायै स्वाहा

oṁ jāmbūnadasamānābhāyai svāhā
She who shines like gold

- 407 -

ॐ जाम्बूनदविभूषणायै स्वाहा

oṁ jāmbūnadavibhūṣaṇāyai svāhā
She who radiates like gold

- 408 -

ॐ जम्भहायै स्वाहा

oṁ jambhahāyai svāhā

She who slays the demon Jambha, the devourer

- 409 -

ॐ जातिदायै स्वाहा

oṁ jātidāyai svāhā

She who gives distinction to all beings born

- 410 -

ॐ जात्यै स्वाहा

oṁ jātyai svāhā

She who is the distinctions among humans

- 411 -

ॐ ज्ञानदायै स्वाहा

oṁ jñānadāyai svāhā

She who gives wisdom

- 412 -

ॐ ज्ञानगोचरायै स्वाहा

oṁ jñānagocarāyai svāhā

She who travels with the light of wisdom

- 413 -

ॐ ज्ञानभायै स्वाहा

oṁ jñānabhāyai svāhā

She who shines with wisdom

- 414 -

ॐ ज्ञानरूपायै स्वाहा

oṁ jñānarūpāyai svāhā

She who is the form of wisdom

- 415 -

ॐ ज्ञानविज्ञानशालिन्यै स्वाहा

oṁ jñānavijñānaśālinyai svāhā

She who is strong in wisdom and its application

- 416 -

ॐ जिनजैत्र्यै स्वाहा

oṁ jinajaitryai svāhā

She who is victorious over the victorious

- 417 -

ॐ जिनधारायै स्वाहा

oṁ jinadhārāyai svāhā

She who supports the victorious

- 418 -

ॐ जिनमात्रे स्वाहा

oṁ jinamātre svāhā

She who is the mother of the victorious

- 419 -

ॐ जिनेश्वर्यै स्वाहा

oṁ jineśvaryai svāhā

She who is the supreme goddess of the victorious

- 420 -

ॐ जितेन्द्रियायै स्वाहा

oṁ jitendriyāyai svāhā

She who has conquered the senses

- 421 -

ॐ जनाधारायै स्वाहा

oṁ janādhārāyai svāhā

She who supports all beings born

- 422 -

ॐ अजिनाम्बरधारिण्यै स्वाहा

oṁ ajināmbaradhāriṇyai svāhā

She who is the mother who supports invincibility

- 423 -

ॐ शम्भुकोटिदुराधरायै स्वाहा

oṁ śambhukoṭidurādharāyai svāhā

She who supports ten million Śivas in the being of peace

- 424 -

ॐ विष्णुकोटिविमर्दिन्यै स्वाहा

oṁ viṣṇukoṭivimardinyai svāhā

She who experiences ten million Viṣṇus

- 425 -

ॐ समुद्रकोटिगम्भीरायै स्वाहा

oṁ samudrakoṭigambhīrāyai svāhā

She who is as passive as ten million oceans

- 426 -

ॐ वायुकोटिमहाबलायै स्वाहा

oṁ vāyukoṭimahābalāyai svāhā

She who has the great strength of ten million winds

- 427 -

ॐ सूर्यकोटिप्रतीकाशायै स्वाहा

oṁ sūryakoṭipratīkāśāyai svāhā

She who illuminates like ten million suns

- 428 -

ॐ यमकोटिदुरापहायै स्वाहा

oṁ yamakoṭidurāpahāyai svāhā

She who takes control like ten million gods of death

- 429 -

ॐ कामधुक्कोटिफलदायै स्वाहा

oṁ kāmadhukkoṭiphaladāyai svāhā

She who gives the fruit of ten million desires

- 430 -

ॐ शक्रकोटिसुराज्यदायै स्वाहा

oṁ śakrakoṭisurājyadāyai svāhā

She who gives dominion like ten million lords of heaven

- 431 -

ॐ कन्दर्पकोटिलावण्यायै स्वाहा

oṁ kandarpakoṭilāvaṇyāyai svāhā

She who has the beauty of ten million gods of love

- 432 -

ॐ पद्मकोटिनिभाननायै स्वाहा

oṁ padmakoṭinibhānanāyai svāhā
She who resembles ten million lotuses

- 433 -

ॐ पृथ्वीकोटिजनाधारायै स्वाहा

oṁ pṛthvīkoṭijanādhārāyai svāhā
She who supports all beings like ten million Earths

- 434 -

ॐ अग्निकोटिभयङ्कर्यै स्वाहा

oṁ agnikoṭibhayaṅkaryai svāhā
She who is as fearful as ten million fires

- 435 -

ॐ अणिमायै स्वाहा

oṁ aṇimāyai svāhā
She who becomes as small as an atom

- 436 -

ॐ महिमायै स्वाहा

oṁ mahimāyai svāhā
She who becomes big

- 437 -

ॐ प्राप्त्यै स्वाहा

oṁ prāptyai svāhā
She who gets

- 438 -

ॐ गरिमायै स्वाहा

oṁ garimāyai svāhā
She who can make herself heavy

- 439 -

ॐ लघिमायै स्वाहा

oṁ laghimāyai svāhā
She who can make herself light

- 440 -

ॐ प्राकाम्यदायै स्वाहा

oṁ prākāmyadāyai svāhā
She who fulfills desire

- 441 -

ॐ वशङ्कर्यै स्वाहा

oṁ vaśaṅkaryai svāhā
She who subjugates all to her will

- 442 -

ॐ ईशिकायै स्वाहा

oṁ īśikāyai svāhā
She who is the master of all

- 443 -

ॐ सिद्धिदायै स्वाहा

oṁ siddhidāyai svāhā
She who gives attainments

- 444 -

ॐ महिमादिगुणोपेतायै स्वाहा

oṁ mahimādiguṇopetāyai svāhā

She who expands attainments like becoming big

- 445 -

ॐ अणिमाद्यष्टसिद्धिदायै स्वाहा

oṁ aṇimādyaṣṭasiddhidāyai svāhā

She who gives the eight attainments like becoming small

- 446 -

ॐ जवनघ्न्यै स्वाहा

oṁ javanaghnyai svāhā

She who moves swiftly

- 447 -

ॐ जनाधीनायै स्वाहा

oṁ janādhīnāyai svāhā

She who generates creation

- 448 -

ॐ जामिन्यै स्वाहा

oṁ jāminyai svāhā

She who has logic

- 449 -

ॐ जरापहायै स्वाहा

oṁ jarāpahāyai svāhā

She who takes away all lethargy

- 450 -

ॐ तारिण्यै स्वाहा

oṁ tāriṇyai svāhā
She who radiates light

- 451 -

ॐ तारिकायै स्वाहा

oṁ tārikāyai svāhā
She who causes illumination

- 452 -

ॐ तारायै स्वाहा

oṁ tārāyai svāhā
She who illuminates

- 453 -

ॐ तोतलायै स्वाहा

oṁ totalāyai svāhā
She who sings like a parrot

- 454 -

ॐ तुलसीप्रियायै स्वाहा

oṁ tulasīpriyāyai svāhā
She who is the beloved tulasi

- 455 -

ॐ तन्त्रिण्यै स्वाहा

oṁ tantriṇyai svāhā
She who is all synthesis

- 456 -

ॐ तन्त्ररूपायै स्वाहा

oṁ tantrarūpāyai svāhā
She who is the form of synthesis

- 457 -

ॐ तन्त्रज्ञायै स्वाहा

oṁ tantrajñāyai svāhā
She who is the knowledge of synthesis

- 458 -

ॐ तन्त्रधारिण्यै स्वाहा

oṁ tantradhāriṇyai svāhā
She who supports synthesis

- 459 -

ॐ तारहारायै स्वाहा

oṁ tārahārāyai svāhā
She who is the illuminator who takes away darkness

- 460 -

ॐ तुळजायै स्वाहा

oṁ tulajāyai svāhā
She who is beyond all comparison

- 461 -

ॐ डाकिनीतन्त्रगोचरायै स्वाहा

oṁ ḍākinītantragocarāyai svāhā
She who travels with the light of the dākinī tantra

- 462 -

ॐ त्रिपुरायै स्वाहा

oṁ tripurāyai svāhā

She who dwells in the three cities

- 463 -

ॐ त्रिदशायै स्वाहा

oṁ tridaśāyai svāhā

She who is the goddess of the thirty gods

- 464 -

ॐ त्रिस्थायै स्वाहा

oṁ tristhāyai svāhā

She who resides in all the threes

- 465 -

ॐ त्रिपुरासुरघातिन्यै स्वाहा

oṁ tripurāsuraghātinyai svāhā

She who destroyed the ruler of duality in the three cities

- 466 -

ॐ त्रिगुणायै स्वाहा

oṁ triguṇāyai svāhā

She who has three qualities

- 467 -

ॐ त्रिकोणस्थायै स्वाहा

oṁ trikoṇasthāyai svāhā

She who resides in the three angles

- 468 -

ॐ त्रिमात्रायै स्वाहा

oṁ trimātrāyai svāhā

She who is the mother of the three

- 469 -

ॐ त्रितसुस्थितायै स्वाहा

oṁ tritasusthitāyai svāhā

She who is situated in the three angles

- 470 -

ॐ त्रैविद्यायै स्वाहा

oṁ traividyāyai svāhā

She who is the knowledge of the three

- 471 -

ॐ त्रय्यै स्वाहा

oṁ trayyai svāhā

She who is three

- 472 -

ॐ त्रिघ्न्यै स्वाहा

oṁ trighnyai svāhā

She who removes the three bonds

- 473 -

ॐ तुरीयायै स्वाहा

oṁ turīyāyai svāhā

She who is beyond

- 474 -

ॐ त्रिपुरेश्वर्यै स्वाहा

oṁ tripureśvaryai svāhā

She who is the supreme ruler of the three cities

- 475 -

ॐ त्रिकोदरस्थायै स्वाहा

oṁ trikodarasthāyai svāhā

She who resides in the threefold digestive power

- 476 -

ॐ त्रिविधायै स्वाहा

oṁ trividhāyai svāhā

She who creates the three divisions

- 477 -

ॐ त्रैलोक्यायै स्वाहा

oṁ trailokyāyai svāhā

She who is the three worlds

- 478 -

ॐ त्रिपुरात्मिकायै स्वाहा

oṁ tripurātmikāyai svāhā

She who is the soul of the three cities

- 479 -

ॐ त्रिधाम्न्यै स्वाहा

oṁ tridhāmnyai svāhā

She who resides in the three dwelling places

- 480 -

ॐ त्रिदशाराध्यायै स्वाहा

oṁ tridaśārādhyāyai svāhā
She who is served by the thirty gods

- 481 -

ॐ त्र्यक्षायै स्वाहा

oṁ tryakṣāyai svāhā
She who is the three letters

- 482 -

ॐ त्रिपुरवासिन्यै स्वाहा

oṁ tripuravāsinyai svāhā
She who dwells in the three cities

- 483 -

ॐ त्रिवर्णायै स्वाहा

oṁ trivarṇāyai svāhā
She who has three colors or castes

- 484 -

ॐ त्रिपद्यै स्वाहा

oṁ tripadyai svāhā
She who has three syllables

- 485 -

ॐ तारायै स्वाहा

oṁ tārāyai svāhā
She who illuminates

- 486 -

ॐ त्रिमूर्तिजनन्यै स्वाहा

oṁ trimūrtijananyai svāhā
She who is the mother of the three deities

- 487 -

ॐ इत्वरायै स्वाहा

oṁ itvarāyai svāhā
She who makes the journey

- 488 -

ॐ त्रिदिवायै स्वाहा

oṁ tridivāyai svāhā
She who is the three divine lights

- 489 -

ॐ त्रिदिवेशायै स्वाहा

oṁ tridiveśāyai svāhā
She who is shown as the three divine lights

- 490 -

ॐ आदिदेव्यै स्वाहा

oṁ ādidevyai svāhā
She who is the foremost goddess

- 491 -

ॐ त्रैलोक्यधारिण्यै स्वाहा

oṁ trailokyadhāriṇyai svāhā
She who supports the three worlds

- 492 -

ॐ त्रिमूर्त्यै स्वाहा

oṁ trimūrtyai svāhā
She who is the three deities

- 493 -

ॐ त्रिजनन्यै स्वाहा

oṁ trijananyai svāhā
She who is the three mothers

- 494 -

ॐ त्रिभुवे स्वाहा

oṁ tribhuve svāhā
She who is the three worlds

- 495 -

ॐ त्रिपुरसुन्दर्यै स्वाहा

oṁ tripurasundaryai svāhā
She who is the beautiful one of three places

- 496 -

ॐ तपस्विन्यै स्वाहा

oṁ tapasvinyai svāhā
She who performs austerities

- 497 -

ॐ तपोनिष्ठायै स्वाहा

oṁ taponiṣṭāyai svāhā
She who is sincere in performing austerities

- 498 -

ॐ तरुण्यै स्वाहा

oṁ taruṇyai svāhā
She who is progressive

- 499 -

ॐताररूपिण्यै स्वाहा

oṁ tārarūpiṇyai svāhā
She who is the form of the illuminator

- 500 -

ॐ तामस्यै स्वाहा

oṁ tāmasyai svāhā
She who is dark

- 501 -

ॐ तापस्यै स्वाहा

oṁ tāpasyai svāhā
She who is light

- 502 -

ॐ तापघ्न्यै स्वाहा

oṁ tāpaghnyai svāhā
She who destroys affliction

- 503 -

ॐ तमोपहायै स्वाहा

oṁ tamopahāyai svāhā
She who takes away darkness

- 504 -

ॐ तरुणार्कप्रतीकाशायै स्वाहा

oṁ taruṇārkapratīkāśāyai svāhā

She who is the illumination of the rising sun

- 505 -

ॐ तप्तकाञ्चनसन्निभायै स्वाहा

oṁ taptakāñcanasannibhāyai svāhā

She who shines like melted gold

- 506 -

ॐ उन्मादिन्यै स्वाहा

oṁ unmādinyai svāhā

She who is crazy

- 507 -

ॐ तन्तुरूपायै स्वाहा

oṁ tanturūpāyai svāhā

She who is the form of the vows of sacrifice

- 508 -

ॐ त्रैलोक्यव्यापिकायै स्वाहा

oṁ trailokyavyāpikāyai svāhā

She who is the well of the three worlds

- 509 -

ॐ ईश्वर्यै स्वाहा

oṁ īśvaryai svāhā

She who is the supreme goddess

- 510 -

ॐ तार्किक्यै स्वाहा

oṁ tārkikyai svāhā

She who is excellent at debate

- 511 -

ॐ तर्क विद्यायै स्वाहा

oṁ tarka vidyāyai svāhā

She who is the knowledge of debate

- 512 -

ॐ तापत्रयविनाशिन्यै स्वाहा

oṁ tāpatrayavināśinyai svāhā

She who destroys the three fires

- 513 -

ॐ त्रिपुष्करायै स्वाहा

oṁ tripuṣkarāyai svāhā

She who is the cause of the three kinds of nourishment

- 514 -

ॐ त्रिकालज्ञायै स्वाहा

oṁ trikālajñāyai svāhā

She who has knowledge of the three times

- 515 -

ॐ त्रिसन्ध्यायै स्वाहा

oṁ trisandhyāyai svāhā

She who is the three times of prayer

- 516 -

ॐ त्रिलोचानायै स्वाहा

oṁ trilocānāyai svāhā
She who has three eyes

- 517 -

ॐ त्रिवर्गायै स्वाहा

oṁ trivargāyai svāhā
She who has three objectives in life

- 518 -

ॐ त्रिवर्गस्थायै स्वाहा

oṁ trivargasthāyai svāhā
She who resides in the three objectives

- 519 -

ॐ तपस्सिद्धिदायिन्यै स्वाहा

oṁ tapassiddhidāyinyai svāhā
She who gives the attainment of austerities

- 520 -

ॐ अधोक्षजायै स्वाहा

oṁ adhokṣajāyai svāhā
She who is born from religious knowledge

- 521 -

ॐ अयोध्यायै स्वाहा

oṁ ayodhyāyai svāhā
She who dwells in Ayodhya

- 522 -

ॐ अपर्णायै स्वाहा

oṁ aparṇāyai svāhā
She who is indivisible

- 523 -

ॐ अवन्तिकायै स्वाहा

oṁ avantikāyai svāhā
She who dwells in Ujjain

- 524 -

ॐ कारिकायै स्वाहा

oṁ kārikāyai svāhā
She who is a concise statement of doctrine

- 525 -

ॐ तीर्थरूपायै स्वाहा

oṁ tīrtharūpāyai svāhā
She who is the form of the pilgrimage places

- 526 -

ॐ तीर्थायै स्वाहा

oṁ tīrthāyai svāhā
She who is a pilgrimage place

- 527 -

ॐ तीर्थकर्यै स्वाहा

oṁ tīrthakaryai svāhā
She who is the effect of a pilgrimage place

- 528 -

ॐ दारिद्र्दुःखदलिन्यै स्वाहा

oṁ dāridraduḥkhadalinyai svāhā
She who removes pain and affliction

- 529 -

ॐ अदीनायै स्वाहा

oṁ adīnāyai svāhā
She who is noble

- 530 -

ॐ दीनवत्सलायै स्वाहा

oṁ dīnavatsalāyai svāhā
She whose children are lowly

- 531 -

ॐ दिनानाथप्रियायै स्वाहा

oṁ dinānāthapriyāyai svāhā
She who is the beloved of the lord of the day

- 532 -

ॐ दीर्घायै स्वाहा

oṁ dīrghāyai svāhā
She who has long life

- 533 -

ॐ दयापूर्णायै स्वाहा

oṁ dayāpūrṇāyai svāhā
She who has perfect compassion

- 534 -

ॐ दयात्मिकायै स्वाहा

oṁ dayātmikāyai svāhā
She who is the soul of compassion

- 535 -

ॐ देवदानवसम्पूज्यायै स्वाहा

oṁ devadānavasampūjyāyai svāhā
She who is worshipped by the gods and asuras

- 536 -

ॐ देवानां प्रियकारिण्यै स्वाहा

oṁ devānāṁ priyakāriṇyai svāhā
She who is the cause of the love of the gods

- 537 -

ॐ दक्षपुत्र्यै स्वाहा

oṁ dakṣaputryai svāhā
She who is the daughter of ability

- 538 -

ॐ दक्षमात्रे स्वाहा

oṁ dakṣamātre svāhā
She who is the mother of ability

- 539 -

ॐ दक्षयज्ञविनाशिन्यै स्वाहा

oṁ dakṣayajñavināśinyai svāhā
She who is the destroyer of Daksha's sacrifice

\- 540 -

ॐ देवसुवे स्वाहा

oṁ devasuve svāhā

She who is the excellent being of the gods

\- 541 -

ॐ दक्षिणायै स्वाहा

oṁ dakṣiṇāyai svāhā

She who is preferred

\- 542 -

ॐ दक्षायै स्वाहा

oṁ dakṣāyai svāhā

She who has ability

\- 543 -

ॐ दुर्गायै स्वाहा

oṁ durgāyai svāhā

She who removes difficulties

\- 544 -

ॐ दुर्गतिनाशिन्यै स्वाहा

oṁ durgatināśinyai svāhā

She who destroys affliction

\- 545 -

ॐ देवकीगर्भसम्भूतायै स्वाहा

oṁ devakīgarbhasambhūtāyai svāhā

She who shines in the womb of Devaki

- 546 -

ॐ दुर्गदैत्यविनाशिन्यै स्वाहा

oṁ durgadaityavināśinyai svāhā

She who destroys the duality of affliction

- 547 -

ॐ अट्टायै स्वाहा

oṁ aṭṭāyai svāhā

She who is lofty

- 548 -

ॐ अट्टहासिन्यै स्वाहा

oṁ aṭṭahāsinyai svāhā

She who dwells on a very high place

- 549 -

ॐ दोलायै स्वाहा

oṁ dolāyai svāhā

She who swings on a swing

- 550 -

ॐ दोलाकर्माभिनन्दिन्यै स्वाहा

oṁ dolākarmābhinandinyai svāhā

She who takes great delight in swinging on a swing

- 551 -

ॐ देवक्यै स्वाहा

oṁ devakyai svāhā

She who is Devaki

- 552 -

ॐ देविकायै स्वाहा

oṁ devikāyai svāhā

She who is the Goddess

- 553 -

ॐ देव्यै स्वाहा

oṁ devyai svāhā

She who is divine

- 554 -

ॐ दुरितघ्न्यै स्वाहा

oṁ duritaghnyai svāhā

She who destroys the wicked

- 555 -

ॐ तड्यै स्वाहा

oṁ taḍyai svāhā

She who strikes like lightning

- 556 -

ॐ गण्डक्यै स्वाहा

oṁ gaṇḍakyai svāhā

She who is obstacles

- 557 -

ॐ गल्लक्यै स्वाहा

oṁ gallakyai svāhā

She who is delicate like crystal

- 558 -

ॐ क्षिप्रायै स्वाहा

oṁ kṣiprāyai svāhā
She who is the Kṣipra River

- 559 -

ॐ द्वारकायै स्वाहा

oṁ dvārakāyai svāhā
She who dwells in Dvārka

- 560 -

ॐ द्वारवत्यै स्वाहा

oṁ dvāravatyai svāhā
She who is the spirit of Dvārka

- 561 -

ॐ अनन्दोदधिमध्यस्थायै स्वाहा

oṁ anandodadhimadhyasthāyai svāhā
She who resides in the midst of blissful waters

- 562 -

ॐ कटिसूत्रैरलङ्कतायै स्वाहा

oṁ kaṭisūtrairalaṅkatāyai svāhā
She who is adorned with a thread at her waist

- 563 -

ॐ घोराग्निदाहदमन्यै स्वाहा

oṁ ghorāgnidāhadamanyai svāhā
She who extinguishes frightening fires

- 564 -

ॐ दुःखदुस्वप्ननाशिन्यै स्वाहा

oṁ duḥkhadusvapnanāśinyai svāhā

She who destroys the pain of bad dreams

- 565 -

ॐ श्रीमय्यै स्वाहा

oṁ śrīmayyai svāhā

She who manifests respect

- 566 -

ॐ श्रीमत्यै स्वाहा

oṁ śrīmatyai svāhā

She who is respected

- 567 -

ॐ श्रेष्ठायै स्वाहा

oṁ śreṣṭāyai svāhā

She who is most excellent

- 568 -

ॐ श्रीकर्यै स्वाहा

oṁ śrīkaryai svāhā

She who is the effect of respect

- 569 -

ॐ श्रीविभविन्यै स्वाहा

oṁ śrīvibhavinyai svāhā

She who has the attitude of respect

- 570 -

ॐ श्रीदायै स्वाहा

oṁ śrīdāyai svāhā
She who gives respect

- 571 -

ॐ श्रीमायै स्वाहा

oṁ śrīmāyai svāhā
She who is the mother of respect

- 572 -

ॐ श्रीनिवासायै स्वाहा

oṁ śrīnivāsāyai svāhā
She who resides in respect

- 573 -

ॐ श्रीमत्यै स्वाहा

oṁ śrīmatyai svāhā
She who is respected

- 574 -

ॐ श्रीयै स्वाहा

oṁ śrīyai svāhā
She who is respect

- 575 -

ॐ श्रीमत्यै स्वाहा

oṁ śrīmatyai svāhā
She who is respected

- 576 -

ॐ गत्ये स्वाहा

oṁ gatye svāhā
She who is the refuge

- 577 -

ॐ धनदायै स्वाहा

oṁ dhanadāyai svāhā
She who is the giver of wealth

- 578 -

ॐ दामिन्यै स्वाहा

oṁ dāminyai svāhā
She who is peace

- 579 -

ॐ दान्तायै स्वाहा

oṁ dāntāyai svāhā
She who has teeth

- 580 -

ॐ धर्मदायै स्वाहा

oṁ dharmadāyai svāhā
She who is the giver of the ideals of perfection

- 581 -

ॐ धनशालिन्यै स्वाहा

oṁ dhanaśālinyai svāhā
She who is extremely wealthy

- 582 -

ॐ दाडिमीपुष्पसङ्काशायै स्वाहा

oṁ dāḍimīpuṣpasaṅkāśāyai svāhā

She who radiates like a pomegranate flower

- 583 -

ॐ धनागारायै स्वाहा

oṁ dhanāgārāyai svāhā

She who is the dwelling place of all wealth

- 584 -

ॐ धनञ्जय्यै स्वाहा

oṁ dhanañjayyai svāhā

She who is victorious over wealth

- 585 -

ॐ धूम्राभायै स्वाहा

oṁ dhūmrābhāyai svāhā

She who shines through the duality of obscure perception

- 586 -

ॐ धूम्रदैत्यघ्न्यै स्वाहा

oṁ dhūmradaityaghnyai svāhā

She who destroys the duality of obscure perception

- 587 -

ॐ धवलायै स्वाहा

oṁ dhavalāyai svāhā

She who is dazzling white

- 588 -

ॐ धवलप्रियायै स्वाहा

oṁ dhavalapriyāyai svāhā
She who loves dazzling white

- 589 -

ॐ धूम्रवक्रायै स्वाहा

oṁ dhūmravakrāyai svāhā
She whose infirmity is obscure

- 590 -

ॐ धूम्रनेत्रायै स्वाहा

oṁ dhūmranetrāyai svāhā
She who has obscure perception

- 591 -

ॐ धूम्रकेश्यै स्वाहा

oṁ dhūmrakeśyai svāhā
She who has smoky hair

- 592 -

ॐ धूसरायै स्वाहा

oṁ dhūsarāyai svāhā
She who is grey

- 593 -

ॐ धरण्यै स्वाहा

oṁ dharaṇyai svāhā
She who is the earth

- 594 -

ॐ धारिण्यै स्वाहा

oṁ dhāriṇyai svāhā

She who supports

- 595 -

ॐ धैर्यायै स्वाहा

oṁ dhairyāyai svāhā

She who has intelligence

- 596 -

ॐ धरायै स्वाहा

oṁ dharāyai svāhā

She who supports

- 597 -

ॐ धात्र्यै स्वाहा

oṁ dhātryai svāhā

She who creates

- 598 -

ॐ धैर्यदायै स्वाहा

oṁ dhairyadāyai svāhā

She who gives endurance

- 599 -

ॐ दमिन्यै स्वाहा

oṁ daminyai svāhā

She who provides a house

- 600 -

ॐ धर्मिण्यै स्वाहा

oṁ dharmiṇyai svāhā
She who is virtuous

- 601 -

ॐ धुरे स्वाहा

oṁ dhure svāhā
She who is foremost

- 602 -

ॐ दयायै स्वाहा

oṁ dayāyai svāhā
She who is compassionate

- 603 -

ॐ दोग्ध्रयै स्वाहा

oṁ dogdhrayai svāhā
She who is a pail full of milk

- 604 -

ॐ दुरासट्टायै स्वाहा

oṁ durāsaṭṭāyai svāhā
She who overcomes difficulties

- 605 -

ॐ नारायण्यै स्वाहा

oṁ nārāyaṇyai svāhā
She who exposes consciousness

- 606 -

ॐ नारसिंह्यै स्वाहा

oṁ nārasiṁhyai svāhā

She who is the energy of the one who is half-man, half-lion

- 607 -

ॐ नृसिंहहृदयालयायै स्वाहा

oṁ nṛsiṁhahṛdayālayāyai svāhā

She who resides in the heart of the one who is half man, half lion

- 608 -

ॐ नागिन्यै स्वाहा

oṁ nāginyai svāhā

She who is a serpent of energy

- 609 -

ॐ नागकन्यायै स्वाहा

oṁ nāgakanyāyai svāhā

She who is the daughter of a serpent of energy

- 610 -

ॐ नागसुवे स्वाहा

oṁ nāgasuve svāhā

She who is the excellent being of a serpent of energy

- 611 -

ॐ नागनायिकायै स्वाहा

oṁ nāganāyikāyai svāhā

She who is the leader of the serpents of energy

- 612 -

ॐ नानारत्नविचित्रांग्यै स्वाहा

oṁ nānāratnavicitrāṁgyai svāhā
She whose body has the image of various jewels

- 613 -

ॐ नानाभरणमण्डितायै स्वाहा

oṁ nānābharaṇamaṇḍitāyai svāhā
She who is adorned with various ornaments

- 614 -

ॐ दुर्गस्थायै स्वाहा

oṁ durgasthāyai svāhā
She who is situated in the reliever of difficulties

- 615 -

ॐ दुर्गरूपायै स्वाहा

oṁ durgarūpāyai svāhā
She who is the form of the reliever of difficulties

- 616 -

ॐ दुःखदुष्कृतनाशिन्यै स्वाहा

oṁ duḥkhaduṣkṛtanāśinyai svāhā
She who destroys the pain of evil deeds

- 617 -

ॐ ह्रींकार्यै स्वाहा

oṁ hrīṁkāryai svāhā
She who is the letter Hriṁ

- 618 -

ॐ श्रींकार्यै स्वाहा

oṁ śrīṁkāryai svāhā
She who is the letter Śriṁ

- 619 -

ॐ हुंकार्यै स्वाहा

oṁ huṁkāryai svāhā
She who is the letter Huṁ

- 620 -

ॐ क्लेशनाशिन्यै स्वाहा

oṁ kleśanāśinyai svāhā
She who destroys all blemishes

- 621 -

ॐ नागात्मजायै स्वाहा

oṁ nāgātmajāyai svāhā
She who gives birth to the soul of the serpent of energy

- 622 -

ॐ नागरर्यै स्वाहा

oṁ nāgararyai svāhā
She who is as knowledgeable as a serpent of energy

- 623 -

ॐ नवीनायै स्वाहा

oṁ navīnāyai svāhā
She who is young

- 624 -

ॐ नूतनप्रियायै स्वाहा

oṁ nūtanapriyāyai svāhā
She who is new love

- 625 -

ॐ नीरजास्यायै स्वाहा

oṁ nīrajāsyāyai svāhā
She who was produced from the waters

- 626 -

ॐ नीरजाभायै स्वाहा

oṁ nīrajābhāyai svāhā
She who shines from the waters

- 627 -

ॐ नवलावण्यसुन्दर्यै स्वाहा

oṁ navalāvaṇyasundaryai svāhā
She who has young, charming beauty

- 628 -

ॐ नीतिज्ञायै स्वाहा

oṁ nītijñāyai svāhā
She who knows discipline

- 629 -

ॐ नीतिदायै स्वाहा

oṁ nītidāyai svāhā
She who gives discipline

- 630 -

ॐ नीत्यै स्वाहा

oṁ nītyai svāhā
She who is discipline

- 631 -

ॐ नीम्ननाभ्यै स्वाहा

oṁ nīmnanābhyai svāhā
She whose belly button is deep

- 632 -

ॐ नागेश्वर्यै स्वाहा

oṁ nāgeśvaryai svāhā
She who is the supreme ruler of the serpents of energy

- 633 -

ॐ निष्ठायै स्वाहा

oṁ niṣṭāyai svāhā
She who is discipline

- 634 -

ॐ नित्यायै स्वाहा

oṁ nityāyai svāhā
She who is eternal

- 635 -

ॐ निरातङ्कायै स्वाहा

oṁ nirātaṅkāyai svāhā
She who is indifferent to various perceptions

- 636 -

ॐ नागयज्ञोपवीततिन्यै स्वाहा

oṁ nāgayajñopavītatinyai svāhā

She who is the sacred stripe on a serpent of energy

- 637 -

ॐ निधिदायै स्वाहा

oṁ nidhidāyai svāhā

She who gives the system

- 638 -

ॐ निधिरूपायै स्वाहा

oṁ nidhirūpāyai svāhā

She who is the form of the system

- 639 -

ॐ निर्गुणायै स्वाहा

oṁ nirguṇāyai svāhā

She who is without qualities

- 640 -

ॐ नरवाहिन्यै स्वाहा

oṁ naravāhinyai svāhā

She who rides upon a man

- 641 -

ॐ नरमांसरतायै स्वाहा

oṁ naramāṁsaratāyai svāhā

She who is pleased with human flesh

- 642 -

ॐ नार्यै स्वाहा

oṁ nāryai svāhā
She who is a woman

- 643 -

ॐ नरमुण्डविभूषणायै स्वाहा

oṁ naramuṇḍavibhūṣaṇāyai svāhā
She who holds a human head

- 644 -

ॐ निराधारायै स्वाहा

oṁ nirādhārāyai svāhā
She who takes away

- 645 -

ॐ निर्विकारायै स्वाहा

oṁ nirvikārāyai svāhā
She who is without a cause

- 646 -

ॐ नुत्यै स्वाहा

oṁ nutyai svāhā
She who is worshipped

- 647 -

ॐ निर्वाणसुन्दर्यै स्वाहा

oṁ nirvāṇasundaryai svāhā
She who is the beauty beyond manifestation

- 648 -

ॐ नरासृक्पानमत्तायै स्वाहा

oṁ narāsṛkpānamattāyai svāhā
She who is delighted by the drink of human blood

- 649 -

ॐ निवैरायै स्वाहा

oṁ nivairāyai svāhā
She who is without hostility

- 650 -

ॐ नागगामिन्यै स्वाहा

oṁ nāgagāminyai svāhā
She who moves with the serpents of energy

- 651 -

ॐ परमायै स्वाहा

oṁ paramāyai svāhā
She who is the supreme manifestation

- 652 -

ॐ प्रमितायै स्वाहा

oṁ pramitāyai svāhā
She who is the measurement

- 653 -

ॐ प्राज्ञायै स्वाहा

oṁ prājñāyai svāhā
She who is primary knowledge

- 654 -

ॐ पार्वत्यै स्वाहा

oṁ pārvatyai svāhā
She who is the daughter of the mountain

- 655 -

ॐ पर्वतात्मजायै स्वाहा

oṁ parvatātmajāyai svāhā
She who gives birth

- 656 -

ॐ पर्वप्रियायै स्वाहा

oṁ parvapriyāyai svāhā
She who is loves the changes of the moon

- 657 -

ॐ पर्वरतायै स्वाहा

oṁ parvaratāyai svāhā
She who manifests the changes of the moon

- 658 -

ॐ पर्वणे स्वाहा

oṁ parvaṇe svāhā
She who is the changes of the moon

- 659 -

ॐ पर्वपावनापालिन्यै स्वाहा

oṁ parvapāvanāpālinyai svāhā
She who protects the pure changes of the moon

- 660 -

ॐ परात्परतरायै स्वाहा

oṁ parātparatarāyai svāhā
She who is higher than the highest

- 661 -

ॐ पूर्वायै स्वाहा

oṁ pūrvāyai svāhā
She who is in the East

- 662 -

ॐ पश्चिमायै स्वाहा

oṁ paścimāyai svāhā
She who is in the West

- 663 -

ॐ पापनाशिन्यै स्वाहा

oṁ pāpanāśinyai svāhā
She who destroys sin

- 664 -

ॐ पशूनां पतिपत्न्यै स्वाहा

oṁ paśūnāṁ patipatnyai svāhā
She who is the husband and wife of all animals

- 665 -

ॐ पतिभक्तिपरायण्यै स्वाहा

oṁ patibhaktiparāyaṇyai svāhā
She who is always devoted to her husband

- 666 -

ॐ परेश्यै स्वाहा

oṁ pareśyai svāhā
She who is the supreme seer

- 667 -

ॐ पारगायै स्वाहा

oṁ pāragāyai svāhā
She who moves beyond

- 668 -

ॐ परायै स्वाहा

oṁ pārāyai svāhā
She who is an outsider

- 669 -

ॐ परंज्योतिस्वरूपिण्यै स्वाहा

oṁ paraṁjyotisvarūpiṇyai svāhā
She who is the intrinsic nature of the highest light

- 670 -

ॐ निष्ठुरायै स्वाहा

oṁ niṣṭurāyai svāhā
She who is hard

- 671 -

ॐ क्रूरहृदयायै स्वाहा

oṁ krūrahṛdayāyai svāhā
She who has fixed her heart

- 672 -

ॐ परासिद्ध्यै स्वाहा

oṁ parāsiddhyai svāhā
She who has the highest attainment

- 673 -

ॐ परागत्यै स्वाहा

oṁ parāgatyai svāhā
She who is the highest refuge

- 674 -

ॐ पशुघ्न्यै स्वाहा

oṁ paśughnyai svāhā
She who slays animalism

- 675 -

ॐ पशुरूपायै स्वाहा

oṁ paśurūpāyai svāhā
She who has the form of an animal

- 676 -

ॐ पशुहायै स्वाहा

oṁ paśuhāyai svāhā
She who slays animalism

- 677 -

ॐ पशुवाहिन्यै स्वाहा

oṁ paśuvāhinyai svāhā
She who rides on an animal

- 678 -

ॐ पित्रे स्वाहा

oṁ pitre svāhā
She who is the ancestor

- 679 -

ॐ मात्रे स्वाहा

oṁ mātre svāhā
She who is the mother

- 680 -

ॐ यन्त्र्यै स्वाहा

oṁ yantryai svāhā
She who is the yantra or tool

- 681 -

ॐ पशुपाशविनाशिन्यै स्वाहा

oṁ paśupāśavināśinyai svāhā
She who destroys the bonds of animalism

- 682 -

ॐ पद्मिन्यै स्वाहा

oṁ padminyai svāhā
She who is like a lotus

- 683 -

ॐ पद्महस्तायै स्वाहा

oṁ padmahastāyai svāhā
She who has a lotus in her hand

- 684 -

ॐ पद्मकिञ्जल्कवासिन्यै स्वाहा

oṁ padmakiñjalkavāsinyai svāhā
She who dwells in a lotus bud

- 685 -

ॐ पद्मवक्रायै स्वाहा

oṁ padmavakrāyai svāhā
She who has a lotus mouth

- 686 -

ॐ पद्माक्ष्यै स्वाहा

oṁ padmākṣyai svāhā
She who has lotus eyes

- 687 -

ॐ पद्मस्थायै स्वाहा

oṁ padmasthāyai svāhā
She who resides in a lotus

- 688 -

ॐ पद्मसम्भवायै स्वाहा

oṁ padmasambhavāyai svāhā
She who exists in a lotus

- 689 -

ॐ पद्मास्यायै स्वाहा

oṁ padmāsyāyai svāhā
She who is of a lotus

\- 690 -

ॐ पञ्चम्यै स्वाहा

oṁ pañcamyai svāhā
She who is the fifth

\- 691 -

ॐ पूर्णायै स्वाहा

oṁ pūrṇāyai svāhā
She who is full, complete and perfect

\- 692 -

ॐ पूर्णपीठनिवासिन्यै स्वाहा

oṁ pūrṇapīṭhanivāsinyai svāhā
She who sits in the perfect pilgrimage place

\- 693 -

ॐ पद्मरागप्रतीकाशायै स्वाहा

oṁ padmarāgapratīkāśāyai svāhā
She who illuminates the movement of the lotus one

\- 694 -

ॐ पाञ्चाल्यै स्वाहा

oṁ pāñcālyai svāhā
She who resides among the five

\- 695 -

ॐ पञ्चमप्रियायै स्वाहा

oṁ pañcamapriyāyai svāhā
She who is beloved of the fire

- 696 -

ॐ परब्रह्मस्वरूपायै स्वाहा

oṁ parabrahmasvarūpāyai svāhā

She who is the intrinsic nature of the supreme divinity

- 697 -

ॐ परब्रह्मनिवासिन्यै स्वाहा

oṁ parabrahmanivāsinyai svāhā

She who dwells with the supreme divinity

- 698 -

ॐ पारमानन्दमुदितायै स्वाहा

oṁ pāramānandamuditāyai svāhā

She who is intoxicated with supreme bliss

- 699 -

ॐ परचक्रनिवाशिन्यै स्वाहा

oṁ paracakranivāśinyai svāhā

She who resides in the highest center of energy

- 700 -

ॐ परेश्यै स्वाहा

oṁ pareśyai svāhā

She who is the greatest seer of all

- 701 -

ॐ परमायै स्वाहा

oṁ paramāyai svāhā

She who is the supreme manifestation

- 702 -

ॐ पृथ्व्यै स्वाहा

oṁ pṛthvyai svāhā
She who is the earth

- 703 -

ॐ पीनतुङ्गपयोधरायै स्वाहा

oṁ pīnatuṅgapayodharāyai svāhā
She who holds a drinking vessel full of milk

- 704 -

ॐ परावरायै स्वाहा

oṁ parāvarāyai svāhā
She who is the supreme blessing

- 705 -

ॐ परायै स्वाहा

oṁ parāyai svāhā
She who is outside

- 706 -

ॐ विद्यायै स्वाहा

oṁ vidyāyai svāhā
She who is knowledge

- 707 -

ॐ परमानन्ददायिन्यै स्वाहा

oṁ paramānandadāyinyai svāhā
She who is the giver of supreme bliss

- 708 -

ॐ पूजायै स्वाहा

oṁ pūjāyai svāhā
She who is worthy of worship

- 709 -

ॐ प्रजावत्यै स्वाहा

oṁ prajāvatyai svāhā
She who is the spirit of all beings born

- 710 -

ॐ पुष्ट्यै स्वाहा

oṁ puṣṭyai svāhā
She who gives nourishment

- 711 -

ॐ पिनाकिपरिकीर्तितायै स्वाहा

oṁ pinākiparikīrtitāyai svāhā
She whose sharp spear is famous

- 712 -

ॐ प्राणहायै स्वाहा

oṁ prāṇahāyai svāhā
She who takes away life force

- 713 -

ॐ प्राणरूपायै स्वाहा

oṁ prāṇarūpāyai svāhā
She who is the form of the life force

- 714 -

ॐ प्राणदायै स्वाहा

oṁ prāṇadāyai svāhā
She who is the giver of life force

- 715 -

ॐ प्रियम्वदायै स्वाहा

oṁ priyamvadāyai svāhā
She who is the giver of love

- 716 -

ॐ फणिभूषायै स्वाहा

oṁ phaṇibhūṣāyai svāhā
She who shines like the serpent of energy

- 717 -

ॐ फणापेश्यै स्वाहा

oṁ phaṇāpeśyai svāhā
She who wears a nose ornament

- 718 -

ॐ फकाराकुण्ठमालिन्यै स्वाहा

oṁ phakārākuṇṭhamālinyai svāhā
She who wears a flowing garland on her neck

- 719 -

ॐ फणिराट्कृतसर्वांग्यै स्वाहा

oṁ phaṇirāṭkṛtasarvāṁgyai svāhā
She who wears serpents of energy upon her body

- 720 -

ॐ फलिभागनिवासिन्यै स्वाहा

oṁ phalibhāganivāsinyai svāhā
She who resides in every part of fruit

- 721 -

ॐ बलभद्रस्यभगिन्यै स्वाहा

oṁ balabhadrasyabhaginyai svāhā
She who is the partner of excellent strength

- 722 -

ॐ बालायै स्वाहा

oṁ bālāyai svāhā
She who is strength

- 723 -

ॐ बालप्रदायिन्यै स्वाहा

oṁ bālapradāyinyai svāhā
She who is the giver of strength

- 724 -

ॐ फल्गुरूपायै स्वाहा

oṁ phalgurūpāyai svāhā
She who has a very small form

- 725 -

ॐ प्रलम्बघ्न्यै स्वाहा

oṁ pralambaghnyai svāhā
She who ends procrastination

- 726 -

ॐ फल्गूत्सवविनोदिन्यै स्वाहा

oṁ phalgūtsavavinodinyai svāhā
She who plays at the Holi festival

- 727 -

ॐ भवान्यै स्वाहा

oṁ bhavānyai svāhā
She who is the mother of existence

- 728 -

ॐ भवपत्न्यै स्वाहा

oṁ bhavapatnyai svāhā
She who is the wife of existence

- 729 -

ॐ भवभीतिहरायै स्वाहा

oṁ bhavabhītiharāyai svāhā
She who takes away the fear of manifested existence

- 730 -

ॐ भवायै स्वाहा

oṁ bhavāyai svāhā
She who is existence

- 731 -

ॐ भवेश्वर्यै स्वाहा

oṁ bhaveśvaryai svāhā
She who is the supreme lord of existence

- 732 -

ॐ भवाराध्यायै स्वाहा

oṁ bhavārādhyāyai svāhā
She who strives to please existence

- 733 -

ॐ भवेश्यै स्वाहा

oṁ bhaveśyai svāhā
She who is the seer of existence

- 734 -

ॐ भवनायिकायै स्वाहा

oṁ bhavanāyikāyai svāhā
She who is the leader of existence

- 735 -

ॐ भवमात्रे स्वाहा

oṁ bhavamātre svāhā
She who is the mother of existence

- 736 -

ॐ भवागम्यायै स्वाहा

oṁ bhavāgamyāyai svāhā
She who is the supreme wealth

- 737 -

ॐ भवकण्टकनाशिन्यै स्वाहा

oṁ bhavakaṇṭakanāśinyai svāhā
She who is the form of wealth

- 738 -

ॐ भवप्रियायै स्वाहा

oṁ bhavapriyāyai svāhā
She who is the beloved of existence

- 739 -

ॐ भवानन्दायै स्वाहा

oṁ bhavānandāyai svāhā
She who is the bliss of existence

- 740 -

ॐ भव्यायै स्वाहा

oṁ bhavyāyai svāhā
She who is the manifestation of existence

- 741 -

ॐ भवमोचन्यै स्वाहा

oṁ bhavamocanyai svāhā
She who annihilates existence

- 742 -

ॐ भावनीयायै स्वाहा

oṁ bhāvanīyāyai svāhā
She who manifests

- 743 -

ॐ भगवत्यै स्वाहा

oṁ bhagavatyai svāhā
She who is the supreme wealth of existence

- 744 -

ॐ भवभारविनाशिन्यै स्वाहा

oṁ bhavabhāravināśinyai svāhā
She who destroys the burdens of existence

- 745 -

ॐ भूतधात्र्यै स्वाहा

oṁ bhūtadhātryai svāhā
She who creates the elements

- 746 -

ॐ भूतेश्यै स्वाहा

oṁ bhūteśyai svāhā
She who is the goddess of the elements

- 747 -

ॐ भूतस्थायै स्वाहा

oṁ bhūtasthāyai svāhā
She who resides in the elements

- 748 -

ॐ भूतरूपिण्यै स्वाहा

oṁ bhūtarūpiṇyai svāhā
She who is the form of the elements

- 749 -

ॐ भूतमात्रे स्वाहा

oṁ bhūtamātre svāhā
She who is the mother of the elements

- 750 -

ॐ भूतघ्न्यै स्वाहा

oṁ bhūtaghnyai svāhā

She who slays disembodied spirits

- 751 -

ॐ भूतपञ्चकवासिन्यै स्वाहा

oṁ bhūtapañcakavāsinyai svāhā

She who resides in the five elements

- 752 -

ॐ भोगोपचारकुशलायै स्वाहा

oṁ bhogopacārakuśalāyai svāhā

She who is happy with the offerings of enjoyment

- 753 -

ॐ भिस्साधात्र्यै स्वाहा

oṁ bhissādhātryai svāhā

She who is the creator of rice

- 754 -

ॐ भूचर्यै स्वाहा

oṁ bhūcaryai svāhā

She who moves in perceivable existence

- 755 -

ॐ भीतिघ्न्यै स्वाहा

oṁ bhītighnyai svāhā

She who destroys fear

- 756 -

ॐ भक्तिगम्यायै स्वाहा

oṁ bhaktigamyāyai svāhā
She who travels with devotion

- 757 -

ॐ भक्तानामार्तिनाशिन्यै स्वाहा

oṁ bhaktānāmārtināśinyai svāhā
She who destroys enemies of those who bow with devotion

- 758 -

ॐ भक्तानुकम्पिन्यै स्वाहा

oṁ bhaktānukampinyai svāhā
She who has the feelings of devotees

- 759 -

ॐ भीमायै स्वाहा

oṁ bhīmāyai svāhā
She who is terrible

- 760 -

ॐ भगिन्यै स्वाहा

oṁ bhaginyai svāhā
She who is wealth

- 761 -

ॐ भगनायिकायै स्वाहा

oṁ bhaganāyikāyai svāhā
She who is the most important wealth

- 762 -

ॐ भगविद्यायै स्वाहा

oṁ bhagavidyāyai svāhā
She who is the knowledge of the wealth

- 763 -

ॐ भगक्लिन्नायै स्वाहा

oṁ bhagaklinnāyai svāhā
She who is the flow of wealth

- 764 -

ॐ भगयोन्यै स्वाहा

oṁ bhagayonyai svāhā
She who is the womb of wealth

- 765 -

ॐ भगप्रदायै स्वाहा

oṁ bhagapradāyai svāhā
She who is the giver of wealth

- 766 -

ॐ भगेश्यै स्वाहा

oṁ bhageśyai svāhā
She who is the supreme ruler of wealth

- 767 -

ॐ भगरूपायै स्वाहा

oṁ bhagarūpāyai svāhā
She who is the form of wealth

- 768 -

ॐ भगगुह्यायै स्वाहा

oṁ bhagaguhyāyai svāhā
She who is hidden wealth

- 769 -

ॐ भगावहायै स्वाहा

oṁ bhagāvahāyai svāhā
She who is the conveyance of wealth

- 770 -

ॐ भगोदर्यै स्वाहा

oṁ bhagodaryai svāhā
She whose wealth increases

- 771 -

ॐ भगानन्दायै स्वाहा

oṁ bhagānandāyai svāhā
She who is the bliss of wealth

- 772 -

ॐ भाग्यदायै स्वाहा

oṁ bhāgyadāyai svāhā
She who is the giver of fate

- 773 -

ॐ भगमालिन्यै स्वाहा

oṁ bhagamālinyai svāhā
She who wears the garland of wealth

- 774 -

ॐ भोगप्रदायै स्वाहा

oṁ bhogapradāyai svāhā

She who is the giver of enjoyment

- 775 -

ॐ भोगवासायै स्वाहा

oṁ bhogavāsāyai svāhā

She who resides in enjoyment

- 776 -

ॐ भोगमूलायै स्वाहा

oṁ bhogamūlāyai svāhā

She who is the root of enjoyment

- 777 -

ॐ भोगिन्यै स्वाहा

oṁ bhoginyai svāhā

She who is the enjoyer of enjoyment

- 778 -

ॐ भेरुण्डायै स्वाहा

oṁ bheruṇḍāyai svāhā

She who inspires awe

- 779 -

ॐ भेदिन्यै स्वाहा

oṁ bhedinyai svāhā

She who has divisions

- 780 -

ॐ भीमायै स्वाहा

oṁ bhīmāyai svāhā
She who is formidable

- 781 -

ॐ भद्रकाल्यै स्वाहा

oṁ bhadrakālyai svāhā
She who is the excellent one beyond time

- 782 -

ॐ भिदोज्झितायै स्वाहा

oṁ bhidojjhitāyai svāhā
She who is the wisdom of discrimination

- 783 -

ॐ भैरव्यै स्वाहा

oṁ bhairavyai svāhā
She who is fearful

- 784 -

ॐ भुवनेशान्यै स्वाहा

oṁ bhuvaneśānyai svāhā
She who is the ruler of Earth

- 785 -

ॐ भुवनायै स्वाहा

oṁ bhuvanāyai svāhā
She who is the Earth

- 786 -

ॐ भुवनेश्वर्यै स्वाहा

oṁ bhuvaneśvaryai svāhā
She who is the supreme ruler of the Earth

- 787 -

ॐ भीमाक्ष्यै स्वाहा

oṁ bhīmākṣyai svāhā
She who has formidable eyes

- 788 -

ॐ भारत्यै स्वाहा

oṁ bhāratyai svāhā
She who shines with wisdom

- 789 -

ॐ भैरवाष्टकसेवितायै स्वाहा

oṁ bhairavāṣṭakasevitāyai svāhā
She who is served by Bhairava and the eight servants

- 790 -

ॐ भास्वरायै स्वाहा

oṁ bhāsvarāyai svāhā
She who has excellent illumination

- 791 -

ॐ भास्वत्यै स्वाहा

oṁ bhāsvatyai svāhā
She who is the spirit of illumination

- 792 -

ॐ भीत्यै स्वाहा

oṁ bhītyai svāhā
She who is fear

- 793 -

ॐ भास्वदुत्तानशालिन्यै स्वाहा

oṁ bhāsvaduttānaśālinyai svāhā
She who is the strength of rising illumination

- 794 -

ॐ भागीरथ्यै स्वाहा

oṁ bhāgīrathyai svāhā
She who is the Ganges

- 795 -

ॐ भोगवत्यै स्वाहा

oṁ bhogavatyai svāhā
She who is the spirit of all enjoyment

- 796 -

ॐ भवघ्न्यै स्वाहा

oṁ bhavaghnyai svāhā
She who destroys existence

- 797 -

ॐ भुवनात्मिकायै स्वाहा

oṁ bhuvanātmikāyai svāhā
She who is the soul of the Earth

- 798 -

ॐ भूतिदायै स्वाहा

oṁ bhūtidāyai svāhā

She who is the giver of the elements

- 799 -

ॐ भूतिरूपायै स्वाहा

oṁ bhūtirūpāyai svāhā

She who is the form of the elements

- 800 -

ॐ भूतस्थायै स्वाहा

oṁ bhūtasthāyai svāhā

She who is situated in the elements

- 801 -

ॐ भूतवर्धिन्यै स्वाहा

oṁ bhūtavardhinyai svāhā

She who distinguishes the elements

- 802 -

ॐ महेश्वर्यै स्वाहा

oṁ maheśvaryai svāhā

She who is the great seer of all

- 803 -

ॐ महामायायै स्वाहा

oṁ mahāmāyāyai svāhā

She who is the great limitation of consciousness

- 804 -

ॐ महातेजायै स्वाहा

oṁ mahātejāyai svāhā
She who is the great light

- 805 -

ॐ महासूर्यै स्वाहा

oṁ mahāsūryai svāhā
She who is the great sun

- 806 -

ॐ महाजिह्वायै स्वाहा

oṁ mahājihvāyai svāhā
She who has a great tongue

- 807 -

ॐ महाल्लोलायै स्वाहा

oṁ mahālolāyai svāhā
She who has a great wagging tongue

- 808 -

ॐ महादंष्ट्रायै स्वाहा

oṁ mahādaṁṣṭrāyai svāhā
She who has great teeth

- 809 -

ॐ महाभुजायै स्वाहा

oṁ mahābhujāyai svāhā
She who has great arms

- 810 -

ॐ महामोहान्धकारघ्न्यै स्वाहा

oṁ mahāmohāndhakāraghnyai svāhā
She who destroys the great darkness

- 811 -

ॐ महामोक्षप्रदायिन्यै स्वाहा

oṁ mahāmokṣapradāyinyai svāhā
She who is the giver of the great liberation

- 812 -

ॐ महादारिद्रशमन्यै स्वाहा

oṁ mahādāridraśamanyai svāhā
She who calms the great affliction

- 813 -

ॐ महाशत्रुविमर्दिन्यै स्वाहा

oṁ mahāśatruvimardinyai svāhā
She who slays the great enemies

- 814 -

ॐ महाशक्त्यै स्वाहा

oṁ mahāśaktyai svāhā
She who is the great energy

- 815 -

ॐ महाज्योतिषे स्वाहा

oṁ mahājyotiṣe svāhā
She who is the great light

- 816 -

ॐ महासुरविमर्दिन्यै स्वाहा

oṁ mahāsuravimardinyai svāhā
She who slays the great duality

- 817 -

ॐ महाकायायै स्वाहा

oṁ mahākāyāyai svāhā
She who has a great body

- 818 -

ॐ महावीर्यायै स्वाहा

oṁ mahāvīryāyai svāhā
She who has great heroism

- 819 -

ॐ महापातकनाशिन्यै स्वाहा

oṁ mahāpātakanāśinyai svāhā
She who destroys great sins

- 820 -

ॐ महारवायै स्वाहा

oṁ mahāravāyai svāhā
She who has the great song

- 821 -

ॐ मन्त्रमर्य्यै स्वाहा

oṁ mantramaryyai svāhā
She who is the manifestation of mantra

- 822 -

ॐ मणिपूरनिवासिन्यै स्वाहा

oṁ maṇipūranivāsinyai svāhā

She who dwells in the manipūra chakra

- 823 -

ॐ मानिन्यै स्वाहा

oṁ māninyai svāhā

She who is all thought

- 824 -

ॐ मानदायै स्वाहा

oṁ mānadāyai svāhā

She who is the giver of thought

- 825 -

ॐ मान्यायै स्वाहा

oṁ mānyāyai svāhā

She who obeys the mind

- 826 -

ॐ मनश्चक्षुरगोचरायै स्वाहा

oṁ manaścakṣuragocarāyai svāhā

She who moves with the eyes and the mind

- 827 -

ॐ माहेन्द्यै स्वाहा

oṁ māhendyai svāhā

She who is the great emblem of devotion

- 828 -

ॐ मधुरायै स्वाहा

oṁ madhurāyai svāhā
She who is sweet

- 829 -

ॐ मायायै स्वाहा

oṁ māyāyai svāhā
She who measures

- 830 -

ॐ महिषासुरमर्दिन्यै स्वाहा

oṁ mahiṣāsuramardinyai svāhā
She who slays the great ruler of duality in the form of a buffalo

- 831 -

ॐ महाकुण्डलिन्यै स्वाहा

oṁ mahākuṇḍalinyai svāhā
She who is the great kuṇḍalini energy

- 832 -

ॐ शकयै स्वाहा

oṁ śakayai svāhā
She who is competent

- 833 -

ॐ महाविभववर्धिन्यै स्वाहा

oṁ mahāvibhavavardhinyai svāhā
She who distinguishes the great existence

\- 834 -

ॐ मानस्यै स्वाहा

oṁ mānasyai svāhā
She who is thoughtful

\- 835 -

ॐ माधव्यै स्वाहा

oṁ mādhavyai svāhā
She who is the Earth

\- 836 -

ॐ मेधायै स्वाहा

oṁ medhāyai svāhā
She who is the intellect of love

\- 837 -

ॐ मतिदायै स्वाहा

oṁ matidāyai svāhā
She who gives devotion

\- 838 -

ॐ मतिधारिण्यै स्वाहा

oṁ matidhāriṇyai svāhā
She who is the supporter of thought

\- 839 -

ॐ मेनकागर्भसम्भूतायै स्वाहा

oṁ menakāgarbhasambhūtāyai svāhā
She who shines in the womb of Menakā

- 840 -

ॐ मेनकाभगिन्यै स्वाहा

oṁ menakābhaginyai svāhā
She who is the good fortune of Menakā

- 841 -

ॐ मत्यै स्वाहा

oṁ matyai svāhā
She who thinks

- 842 -

ॐ महोदर्यै स्वाहा

oṁ mahodaryai svāhā
She who has a large belly

- 843 -

ॐ मुक्तकेश्यै स्वाहा

oṁ muktakeśyai svāhā
She who has loose hair

- 844 -

ॐ मुक्तिकाम्यार्थसिद्धिदायै स्वाहा

oṁ muktikāmyārthasiddhidāyai svāhā
She who is the giver of attainment of liberation

- 845 -

ॐ महेश्यै स्वाहा

oṁ maheśyai svāhā
She who is the great seer of all

- 846 -

ॐ महिषारूढायै स्वाहा

oṁ mahiṣārūḍhāyai svāhā
She who rides upon a buffalo

- 847 -

ॐ मधुदैत्यविमर्दिन्यै स्वाहा

oṁ madhudaityavimardinyai svāhā
She who is the slayer of the demon Too Much

- 848 -

ॐ महाव्रतायै स्वाहा

oṁ mahāvratāyai svāhā
She who is the great vow

- 849 -

ॐ महामूर्धायै स्वाहा

oṁ mahāmūrdhāyai svāhā
She who has a great head

- 850 -

ॐ महाभयविनाशिन्यै स्वाहा

oṁ mahābhayavināśinyai svāhā
She who is the destroyer of the great fear

- 851 -

ॐ मातङ्गयै स्वाहा

oṁ mātaṅgayai svāhā
She who is the limbs of thought

- 852 -

ॐ मत्तमातङ्गयै स्वाहा

oṁ mattamātaṅgayai svāhā
She who is intoxicated with the limbs of thought

- 853 -

ॐ मातङ्गकुलमण्डितायै स्वाहा

oṁ mātaṅgakulamaṇḍitāyai svāhā
She who contemplates the family of the limbs of thought

- 854 -

ॐ महाघोरायै स्वाहा

oṁ mahāghorāyai svāhā
She who is very fearful

- 855 -

ॐ माननीयायै स्वाहा

oṁ mānanīyāyai svāhā
She who obeys the mind

- 856 -

ॐ मत्तमातङ्गगामिन्यै स्वाहा

oṁ mattamātaṅgagāminyai svāhā
She who moves intoxicated with the limbs of thought

- 857 -

ॐ मुक्ताहारलतोपेतायै स्वाहा

oṁ muktāhāralatopetāyai svāhā
She who has a necklace of pearls

- 858 -

ॐ मदघूर्णितलोचनायै स्वाहा

oṁ madadhūrṇitalocanāyai svāhā
She who has cunning eyes full of love

- 859 -

ॐ महापराधाशिघ्न्यै स्वाहा

oṁ mahāparādhāśighnyai svāhā
She who destroys the greatest faults

- 860 -

ॐ महाचौरभयापहायै स्वाहा

oṁ mahācaurabhayāpahāyai svāhā
She who takes away fear of the greatest thieves

- 861 -

ॐ महाचिन्त्यस्वरूपायै स्वाहा

oṁ mahācintyasvarūpāyai svāhā
She who is the intrinsic nature of the greatest contemplation

- 862 -

ॐ मणिमन्त्रमहौषध्यै स्वाहा

oṁ maṇimantramahauṣadhyai svāhā
She who is the gem of the mantra that is the greatest medicine

- 863 -

ॐ मणिमण्डपमध्यस्थायै स्वाहा

oṁ maṇimaṇḍapamadhyasthāyai svāhā
She who is situated in the middle of the temple of gems

- 864 -

ॐ मणिमालाविराजितायै स्वाहा

oṁ maṇimālāvirājitāyai svāhā

She who is seated upon the garland of gems

- 865 -

ॐ मन्त्रात्मिकायै स्वाहा

oṁ mantrātmikāyai svāhā

She who is the soul of mantras

- 866 -

ॐ मन्त्रगम्यायै स्वाहा

oṁ mantragamyāyai svāhā

She who travels with mantras

- 867 -

ॐ मन्त्रमात्रे स्वाहा

oṁ mantramātre svāhā

She who is the mother of mantras

- 868 -

ॐ सुमन्त्रिण्यै स्वाहा

oṁ sumantriṇyai svāhā

She who is an excellent mantra

- 869 -

ॐ मेरुमन्दरमध्यस्थायै स्वाहा

oṁ merumandaramadhyasthāyai svāhā

She who resides in the midst of Meru Mountain

- 870 -

ॐ मकराकृतिकुण्डलायै स्वाहा

oṁ makarākṛtikuṇḍalāyai svāhā

She who has created the place of crocodiles and sharks

- 871 -

ॐ मन्थरायै स्वाहा

oṁ mantharāyai svāhā

She who gives churning to the mind

- 872 -

ॐ महासूक्ष्मायै स्वाहा

oṁ mahāsūkṣmāyai svāhā

She who is greatly subtle

- 873 -

ॐ महादूत्यै स्वाहा

oṁ mahādūtyai svāhā

She who is the great ambassador

- 874 -

ॐ महेश्वर्यै स्वाहा

oṁ maheśvaryai svāhā

She who is the great seer of all

- 875 -

ॐ मालिन्यै स्वाहा

oṁ mālinyai svāhā

She who cultivates

- 876 -

ॐ मानव्यै स्वाहा

oṁ mānavyai svāhā
She who is human

- 877 -

ॐ माध्व्यै स्वाहा

oṁ mādhvyai svāhā
She who is the Earth

- 878 -

ॐ मदरूपायै स्वाहा

oṁ madarūpāyai svāhā
She who is the form of intoxication

- 879 -

ॐ मदोत्कटायै स्वाहा

oṁ madotkaṭāyai svāhā
She who has immense love

- 880 -

ॐ मदिरायै स्वाहा

oṁ madirāyai svāhā
She who is intoxicating spirit

- 881 -

ॐ मधुरायै स्वाहा

oṁ madhurāyai svāhā
She who is as sweet as honey

- 882 -

ॐ मोदिन्यै स्वाहा

oṁ modinyai svāhā

She who infatuates

- 883 -

ॐ महोक्षितायै स्वाहा

oṁ mahokṣitāyai svāhā

She who has the great strength

- 884 -

ॐ मङ्गलायै स्वाहा

oṁ maṅgalāyai svāhā

She who is welfare

- 885 -

ॐ मधुमय्यै स्वाहा

oṁ madhumayyai svāhā

She who is the manifestation of sweetness

- 886 -

ॐ मधुपानपरायणायै स्वाहा

oṁ madhupānaparāyaṇāyai svāhā

She who always drinks honey

- 887 -

ॐ मनोरमायै स्वाहा

oṁ manoramāyai svāhā

She who is beautiful

- 888 -

ॐ रमायै स्वाहा

oṁ ramāyai svāhā
She who is lovely

- 889 -

ॐ राजराजेश्वर्यै स्वाहा

oṁ rājarājeśvaryai svāhā
She who is the queen of queens

- 890 -

ॐ रमायै स्वाहा

oṁ ramāyai svāhā
She who is lovely

- 891 -

ॐ राजमान्यायै स्वाहा

oṁ rājamānyāyai svāhā
She who obeys the king

- 892 -

ॐ राजपूज्यायै स्वाहा

oṁ rājapūjyāyai svāhā
She who is worshipped by the king

- 893 -

ॐ रक्तोत्पलविभूषणायै स्वाहा

oṁ raktotpalavibhūṣaṇāyai svāhā
She who shines with red

- 894 -

ॐ राजीवलोचनायै स्वाहा

oṁ rājīvalocanāyai svāhā
She who has kingly eyes

- 895 -

ॐ रामायै स्वाहा

oṁ rāmāyai svāhā
She who manifests perfection in the subtle body of consciousness

- 896 -

ॐ राधिकायै स्वाहा

oṁ rādhikāyai svāhā
She who is Rādha

- 897 -

ॐ रामवल्लभायै स्वाहा

oṁ rāmavallabhāyai svāhā
She who is the strength of Rāma (Sītā)

- 898 -

ॐ शाकिन्यै स्वाहा

oṁ śākinyai svāhā
She who is a śākini, an energy for positive change

- 899 -

ॐ डाकिन्यै स्वाहा

oṁ ḍākinyai svāhā
She who is a ḍākini, an energy for negative change

- 900 -

ॐ लावण्याम्बुधिवीचिकायै स्वाहा

oṁ lāvaṇyāmbudhivīcikāyai svāhā
She who fills consciousness with a loving intellect

- 901 -

ॐ रुद्राण्यै स्वाहा

oṁ rudrāṇyai svāhā
She who takes away the tears

- 902 -

ॐ रुद्ररूपायै स्वाहा

oṁ rudrarūpāyai svāhā
She who is the form of He who takes away the tears

- 903 -

ॐ रौद्रायै स्वाहा

oṁ raudrāyai svāhā
She who is fearful

- 904 -

ॐ रुद्रार्तिनाशिन्यै स्वाहा

oṁ rudrārtināśinyai svāhā
She who destroys the enemies of He who takes away the tears

- 905 -

ॐ रक्तप्रियायै स्वाहा

oṁ raktapriyāyai svāhā
She who is the beloved of passion

- 906 -

ॐ रक्तवस्त्रायै स्वाहा

oṁ raktavastrāyai svāhā
She who wears red

- 907 -

ॐ रक्ताक्ष्यै स्वाहा

oṁ raktākṣyai svāhā
She who has red eyes

- 908 -

ॐ रक्तलोचनायै स्वाहा

oṁ raktalocanāyai svāhā
She who has red eyes

- 909 -

ॐ रक्तकेश्यै स्वाहा

oṁ raktakeśyai svāhā
She who has red hair

- 910 -

ॐ रक्तदंष्ट्रायै स्वाहा

oṁ raktadaṁṣṭrāyai svāhā
She who has red teeth

- 911 -

ॐ रक्तचन्दनचर्चितायै स्वाहा

oṁ raktacandanacarcitāyai svāhā
She who wears red sandal paste

- 912 -

ॐ रक्ताङ्ग्यै स्वाहा

oṁ raktāṅgyai svāhā
She who has red limbs

- 913 -

ॐ रक्तभूषायै स्वाहा

oṁ raktabhūṣāyai svāhā
She who shines with red

- 914 -

ॐ रक्तबीजनिपातिन्यै स्वाहा

oṁ raktabījanipātinyai svāhā
She who drinks the seeds of desire

- 915 -

ॐ रागादिदोषरहितायै स्वाहा

oṁ rāgādidoṣarahitāyai svāhā
She who controls anger and other faults

- 916 -

ॐ रतिजायै स्वाहा

oṁ ratijāyai svāhā
She who has conquered spring

- 917 -

ॐ रतिदायिन्यै स्वाहा

oṁ ratidāyinyai svāhā
She who gives the spring

- 918 -

ॐ विश्वेश्वर्यै स्वाहा

oṁ viśveśvaryai svāhā

She who is the supreme lord of the universe

- 919 -

ॐ विशालाक्ष्यै स्वाहा

oṁ viśālākṣyai svāhā

She who has big eyes

- 920 -

ॐ विन्ध्यपीठनिवासिन्यै स्वाहा

oṁ vindhyapīṭhanivāsinyai svāhā

She who resides in the pilgrimage place of the knowledge that bestows humility

- 921 -

ॐ विश्वभुवे स्वाहा

oṁ viśvabhuve svāhā

She who is the being of the universe

- 922 -

ॐ वीरविद्यायै स्वाहा

oṁ vīravidyāyai svāhā

She who is the knowledge of heroism

- 923 -

ॐ वीरसवे स्वाहा

oṁ vīrasave svāhā

She who is excellent heroism

- 924 -

ॐ वीरनन्दिन्यै स्वाहा

oṁ vīranandinyai svāhā
She who is the bliss of heroism

- 925 -

ॐ वीरेश्वर्यै स्वाहा

oṁ vīreśvaryai svāhā
She who is the supreme lord of heroes

- 926 -

ॐ विशालाक्ष्यै स्वाहा

oṁ viśālākṣyai svāhā
She who has big eyes

- 927 -

ॐ विष्णुमायाविमोहिन्यै स्वाहा

oṁ viṣṇumāyāvimohinyai svāhā
She who is mesmerized by Viṣṇu's maya

- 928 -

ॐ विद्याव्यै स्वाहा

oṁ vidyāvyai svāhā
She who is knowledge

- 929 -

ॐ विष्णुरूपायै स्वाहा

oṁ viṣṇurūpāyai svāhā
She who is the form of Viṣṇu

- 930 -

ॐ विशालनयनोत्पलायै स्वाहा

oṁ viśālanayanotpalāyai svāhā

She whose great eyes see above

- 931 -

ॐ विष्णुमात्रे स्वाहा

oṁ viṣṇumātre svāhā

She who is the mother of Viṣṇu

- 932 -

ॐ विश्वात्मने स्वाहा

oṁ viśvātmane svāhā

She who is the soul of the universe

- 933 -

ॐ विष्णुजायास्वरूपिण्यै स्वाहा

oṁ viṣṇujāyāsvarūpiṇyai svāhā

She who is the intrinsic nature that gives birth to Viṣṇu

- 934 -

ॐ ब्रह्मेश्यै स्वाहा

oṁ brahmeśyai svāhā

She who is the supreme lord of the supreme divinity

- 935 -

ॐ ब्रह्मदायै स्वाहा

oṁ brahmadāyai svāhā

She who is the giver of supreme divinity

- 936 -

ॐ ब्राह्म्यै स्वाहा

oṁ brāhmyai svāhā

She who is the energy of supreme divinity

- 937 -

ॐ ब्रह्मण्यै स्वाहा

oṁ brahmaṇyai svāhā

She who knows the intrinsic nature

- 938 -

ॐ ब्रह्मरूपिण्यै स्वाहा

oṁ brahmarūpiṇyai svāhā

She who is the intrinsic nature of supreme divinity

- 939 -

ॐ ब्रह्मेश्यै स्वाहा

oṁ brahmeśyai svāhā

She who is the supreme ruler of supreme divinity

- 940 -

ॐ द्वारकायै स्वाहा

oṁ dvārakāyai svāhā

She who is in Dvaraka

- 941 -

ॐ विश्ववन्द्यायै स्वाहा

oṁ viśvavandyāyai svāhā

She who is worshipped by the universe

- 942 -

ॐ विश्वपाशविमोचन्यै स्वाहा

oṁ viśvapāśavimocanyai svāhā
She who destroys the bonds of the universe

- 943 -

ॐ विश्वासकारिण्यै स्वाहा

oṁ viśvāsakāriṇyai svāhā
She who is the cause of the universe

- 944 -

ॐ विश्ववायै स्वाहा

oṁ viśvavāyai svāhā
She who is the universe

- 945 -

ॐ विश्वशकीर्त्यै स्वाहा

oṁ viśvaśakīrtyai svāhā
She who is the most famous in the universe

- 946 -

ॐ विचक्षणायै स्वाहा

oṁ vicakṣaṇāyai svāhā
She who perceives clearly

- 947 -

ॐ बाणचापधरायै स्वाहा

oṁ bāṇacāpadharāyai svāhā
She who holds a bow and arrows

- 948 -

ॐ वीरायै स्वाहा

oṁ vīrāyai svāhā
She who is a hero

- 949 -

ॐ बिन्दुस्थायै स्वाहा

oṁ bindusthāyai svāhā
She who is situated in the bindu

- 950 -

ॐ बिन्दुमालिन्यै स्वाहा

oṁ bindumālinyai svāhā
She who cultivates the bindu

- 951 -

ॐ षट्चक्रभेदिन्यै स्वाहा

oṁ ṣaṭcakrabhedinyai svāhā
She who pierces the six centers of energy

- 952 -

ॐ षोडायै स्वाहा

oṁ ṣoḍāyai svāhā
She who is the sixteen

- 953 -

ॐ षोडशारनिवासिन्यै स्वाहा

oṁ ṣoḍaśāranivāsinyai svāhā
She who dwells in the sixteen

- 954 -

ॐ शितिकण्ठप्रियायै स्वाहा

oṁ śitikaṇṭhapriyāyai svāhā

She who is the beloved of the one with a dark throat

- 955 -

ॐ शान्तायै स्वाहा

oṁ śāntāyai svāhā

She who is peace

- 956 -

ॐ शाकिन्यै स्वाहा

oṁ śākinyai svāhā

She who is internal peace

- 957 -

ॐ वातरूपिण्यै स्वाहा

oṁ vātarūpiṇyai svāhā

She who is the intrinsic nature of wind

- 958 -

ॐ शाश्वत्यै स्वाहा

oṁ śāśvatyai svāhā

She who is eternal

- 959 -

ॐ शम्भुवनितायै स्वाहा

oṁ śambhuvanitāyai svāhā

She who is the humility of Śambhu

- 960 -

ॐ शाम्भव्यै स्वाहा

oṁ śāmbhavyai svāhā
She who radiates peace

- 961 -

ॐ शिवरूपिण्यै स्वाहा

oṁ śivarūpiṇyai svāhā
She who is the intrinsic nature of Śiva

- 962 -

ॐ शिवमात्रे स्वाहा

oṁ śivamātre svāhā
She who is the mother of Śiva

- 963 -

ॐ शिवदायै स्वाहा

oṁ śivadāyai svāhā
She who is the giver of Śiva

- 964 -

ॐ शिवायै स्वाहा

oṁ śivāyai svāhā
She who is the energy of Śiva

- 965 -

ॐ शिवहृदासनायै स्वाहा

oṁ śivahṛdāsanāyai svāhā
She who sits in the heart of Śiva

- 966 -

ॐ शुक्लाम्बरायै स्वाहा

oṁ śuklāmbarāyai svāhā
She who is clothed in light colors

- 967 -

ॐ शीतलायै स्वाहा

oṁ śītalāyai svāhā
She who is cool

- 968 -

ॐ शीलायै स्वाहा

oṁ śīlāyai svāhā
She who is firm

- 969 -

ॐ शीलप्रदायिन्यै स्वाहा

oṁ śīlapradāyinyai svāhā
She who gives firmness

- 970 -

ॐ शुकप्रियायै स्वाहा

oṁ śukapriyāyai svāhā
She who is the beloved of parrots

- 971 -

ॐ वैद्यविद्यायै स्वाहा

oṁ vaidyavidyāyai svāhā
She who is the knowledge of healing

- 972 -

ॐ सालग्रामशिलायै स्वाहा

oṁ sālagrāmaśilāyai svāhā

She who is the stone that represents Viṣṇu

- 973 -

ॐ शुचये स्वाहा

oṁ śucaye svāhā

She who is purity

- 974 -

ॐ हरिप्रियायै स्वाहा

oṁ haripriyāyai svāhā

She who is the beloved of Hari

- 975 -

ॐ हरमूर्त्यै स्वाहा

oṁ haramūrtyai svāhā

She who is the image that takes away

- 976 -

ॐ हरिनेत्रकृतालयायै स्वाहा

oṁ harinetrakṛtālayāyai svāhā

She who opens and closes the eyes of God

- 977 -

ॐ हरिवक्त्रोद्भवायै स्वाहा

oṁ harivaktrodbhavāyai svāhā

She who is the attitude of the words of God

- 978 -

ॐ हालायै स्वाहा

oṁ hālāyai svāhā
She who destroys

- 979 -

ॐ हरिवक्षस्थलस्थितायै स्वाहा

oṁ harivakṣasthalasthitāyai svāhā
She who is situated in the breast of God

- 980 -

ॐ क्षेमङ्कर्यै स्वाहा

oṁ kṣemaṅkaryai svāhā
She who is prosperous

- 981 -

ॐ क्षित्यै स्वाहा

oṁ kṣityai svāhā
She who is the earth

- 982 -

ॐ क्षेत्रायै स्वाहा

oṁ kṣetrāyai svāhā
She who is the field

- 983 -

ॐ क्षुधितस्य प्रपूरण्यै स्वाहा

oṁ kṣudhitasya prapūraṇyai svāhā
She who fills the hungry

- 984 -

ॐ वैश्यायै स्वाहा

oṁ vaiśyāyai svāhā
She who engages in business

- 985 -

ॐ क्षत्रियायै स्वाहा

oṁ kṣatriyāyai svāhā
She who administrates and defends the people

- 986 -

ॐ शूद्र्यै स्वाहा

oṁ śūdryai svāhā
She who serves the people

- 987 -

ॐ क्षत्रियाणां कुलेश्वर्यै स्वाहा

oṁ kṣatriyāṇāṁ kuleśvaryai svāhā
She who is the supreme ruler of the family of defenders

- 988 -

ॐ हरपत्न्यै स्वाहा

oṁ harapatnyai svāhā
She who is the wife of Śiva

- 989 -

ॐ हराराध्यायै स्वाहा

oṁ harārādhyāyai svāhā
She who is pleased by Śiva

\- 990 -

ॐ हरसुवे स्वाहा

oṁ harasuve svāhā

She whose being is in Śiva

\- 991 -

ॐ हररूपिण्यै स्वाहा

oṁ hararūpiṇyai svāhā

She who is the form of who takes away

\- 992 -

ॐ सर्वानन्दमय्यै स्वाहा

oṁ sarvānandamayyai svāhā

She who is the manifestation of all bliss

\- 993 -

ॐ आनन्दमय्यै स्वाहा

oṁ ānandamayyai svāhā

She who is the manifestation of bliss

\- 994 -

ॐ सिद्धयै स्वाहा

oṁ siddhayai svāhā

She who is attainment

\- 995 -

ॐ सर्वरक्षास्वरूपिण्यै स्वाहा

oṁ sarvarakṣāsvarūpiṇyai svāhā

She who is the intrinsic nature of all protection

- 996 -

ॐ सर्वदुष्टप्रशमन्यै स्वाहा

oṁ sarvaduṣṭapraśamanyai svāhā
She who is the destroyer of all evil

- 997 -

ॐ सर्वेप्सितफलप्रदायै स्वाहा

oṁ sarvepsitaphalapradāyai svāhā
She who is the giver of all fruits

- 998 -

ॐ सर्वसिद्धेश्वराराध्यायै स्वाहा

oṁ sarvasiddheśvarārādhyāyai svāhā
She who is pleased by the supreme lord of all

- 999 -

ॐ ईश्वराध्यायै स्वाहा

oṁ īśvarādhyāyai svāhā
She who is studied by supreme divinity

- 1000 -

ॐ सर्वमङ्गलमङ्गलायै स्वाहा

oṁ sarvamaṅgalamaṅgalāyai svāhā
She who is all the welfare of all the welfare

ॐ नमः इति

oṁ namaḥ iti
Oṁ We bow to the completion

॥ श्री अन्नपूर्णा सहस्र-नामावली समाप्ताः ॥

॥ śrī annapūrṇāsahasra-nāmāvalī samāptāḥ ॥
That is the end of the thousand names of the respected Goddess Annapūrṇā.

श्री अन्नपूर्णास्तोत्रम्

śrī annapūrṇāstotram

\- 1 -

नित्यानन्दकरी वराभयकरी सौन्दर्यरत्नाकरी
निर्धूताऽखिलघोरपावनकरी प्रत्यक्षमाहेश्वरी ।
प्रालेयाचलवंशपावनकरी काशीपुराधीश्वरी
भिक्षां देहि कृपावलम्बनकरी माताऽन्नपूर्णेश्वरी ॥

nityānandakarī varābhayakarī saundaryaratnākarī
nirdhūtā-khilaghorapāvanakarī pratyakṣamāheśvarī
prāleyācalavaṁśapāvanakarī kāśīpurādhīśvarī
bhikṣāṁ dehi kṛpāvalambanakarī
mātā-nnapūrṇeśvarīī

You are the cause of eternal bliss, you grant the boon of freedom from fear, you give the most beautiful jewels. You are unshaken, you purify the great sins of humanity, you are the actual perceivable form of the great goddess. In the great dissolution you purify the family of the mountain. Supreme Goddess of the City of Kāśī, be gracious without delay and grant me alms, Supreme Goddess, Mother Annapūrṇā.

\- 2 -

नानारत्नविचित्रभूषणकरी हेमाम्बराडम्बरी
मुक्ताहारविलम्बमानविलंसद्वक्षोज-कुम्भान्तरी ।
काश्मीरागुरुवासिता रुचिकरी काशीपुराधीश्वरी
भिक्षां देहि कृपावलम्बनकरी माताऽन्नपूर्णेश्वरी ॥

nānāratnavicitrabhūṣaṇakarī hemāmbarāḍambarī
muktāhāravilambamānavilaṁsad
vakṣoj-kumbhāntarī
kāśamīrāguruvāsitā rucikarī kāśīpurādhīśvarī
bhikṣāṁ dehi kṛpāvalambanakarī
mātā-nnapūrṇeśvarī

You are dressed in various jewels and ornaments, wearing a golden cloth, a necklace of pearls adorns your breast. The beautiful fragrance of Kashmir musk emanates from you. Supreme Goddess of the City of Kāśī, be gracious without delay and grant me alms, Supreme Goddess, Mother Annapūrṇā

- 3 -

योगानन्दकरी रिपुक्षयकरी धर्माऽर्थनिष्ठाकरी
चन्द्रार्कानलभासमानलहरी त्रैलोक्यरक्षाकरी ।
सर्वैश्वर्यसमस्तवाञ्छितकरी काशीपुराधीश्वरी
भिक्षां देहि कृपावलम्बनकरी माताऽन्नपूर्णेश्वरी ॥

yogānandakarī ripukṣayakarī dharmā-rthaniṣṭākarī
candrārkānalabhāsamānalaharī trailokyarakṣākarī
sarvaiśvaryasamastavāñchitakarī kāśīpurādhīśvarī
bhikṣāṁ dehi kṛpāvalambanakarī
mātā-nnapūrṇeśvarī

You give the bliss of union, you destroy all limitations and inspire sincerity in Dharma (the ideal of perfection) and artha (the materials necessary to attaining the ideal). The moon, sun and fire, illuminate you who protects the three worlds. Without a doubt you grant all that is imperishable. Supreme Goddess of the City of Kāśī, be gracious without delay and grant me alms, Supreme Goddess, Mother Annapūrṇā.

- 4 -

कैलासाचलकन्दरालयकरी गौरी उमा शङ्करी
कौमारीनिगमार्थ-गोचरकरी ओङ्कारबीजाक्षरी ।
मोक्षद्वारकपाटपाटनकरी काशीपुराधीश्वरी
भिक्षां देहि कृपावलम्बनकरी माताऽन्नपूर्णेश्वरी ॥

kailāsācalakandarālayakarī gaurī umā śaṅkarī kaumārīnigamārtha-gocarakarī oṅkārabījākṣarī mokṣadvārakapāṭapāṭanakarī kāśīpurādhīśvarī bhikṣāṁ dehi kṛpāvalambanakarī mātā-nnapūrṇeśvarī

You dwell in the cave upon Mount Kailāsa and are called She Who is Rays or Light, Mother of Existence, Cause of Peace and Ever Pure One. You make known the hidden meanings of bīja letter Oṁ. You open the doors to liberation. Supreme Goddess of the City of Kāśī, be gracious without delay and grant me alms, Supreme Goddess, Mother Annapūrṇā.

- 5 -

दृश्यादृश्य-प्रभूतवाहनकरी ब्रह्माण्डभाण्डोदरी
लीलानाटकसूत्रभेदनकरी विज्ञानदीपाङ्कुरी ।
श्रीविश्वेशमनःप्रसादनकरी काशीपुराधीश्वरी
भिक्षां देहि कृपावलम्बनकरी माताऽन्नपूर्णेश्वरी ॥

dṛśyādṛśya-prabhūtavāhanakarī brahmāṇḍabhāṇḍodarī līlānāṭakasūtrabhedanakarī vijñānadīpāṅkurī śrīvaśveśamanaḥprasādanakarī kāśīpurādhīśvarī bhikṣāṁ dehi kṛpāvalambanakarī mātā-nnapūrṇeśvarī

You are the Supreme Lord of the perceivable and inperceivable world, of the entire creation and all phenomena within. You bind all beings in the drama of the divine play. You illuminate the light of knowledge and distribute the prasād of the respected universal mind. Supreme Goddess of the City of Kāśī, be gracious without delay and grant me alms, Supreme Goddess, Mother Annapūrṇā.

- 6 -

उर्वीसर्वजनेश्वरी भगवती माताऽन्नपूर्णेश्वरी
वेणीनीलसमानकुन्तलहरी नित्यान्नदानेश्वरी ।
सर्वानन्दकरी दशाशुभकरी काशीपुराधीश्वरी
भिक्षां देहि कृपावलम्बनकरी माताऽन्नपूर्णेश्वरी ॥

urvīsarvajaneśvarī bhagavatī mātā-nnapūrṇeśvarī
veṇīnīlasamānakuntalaharī nityānandāneśvarī
sarvānandakarī daśāśubhakarī kāśīpurādhīśvarī
bhikṣāṁ dehi kṛpāvalambanakarī
mātā-nnapūrṇeśvarī

Goddess of all existence, supreme ruler of all beings born, Supreme Goddess, Mother Annapūrṇā, your braids of hair appear to be dark blue, oh Supreme Goddess, who gives eternal delight. You cause all bliss and make destiny propitious. Supreme Goddess of the City of Kāśī, be gracious without delay and grant me alms, Supreme Goddess, Mother Annapūrṇā.

- 7 -

आदिक्षान्तसमस्तवर्णनकरी शम्भोस्त्रिभावाकरी
काश्मीरा त्रिजनेश्वरी त्रिलहरी नित्याङ्कुरा शर्वरी ।
कामाकांक्षकरी जनोदयकरी काशीपुराधीश्वरी
भिक्षां देहि कृपावलम्बनकरी माताऽन्नपूर्णेश्वरी ॥

ādikṣāntasamastavarṇanakarī śambhostribhāvākarī
kāśmīrā trijaneśvarī trilaharī nityāṅkurā śarvarī
kāmākāṁkṣakarī janodayakarī kāśīpurādhīśvarī
bhikṣāṁ dehi kṛpāvalambanakarī
mātā-nnapūrṇeśvarī

You create all the letters from the beginning (A) to the end (Kṣa). You are the three attitudes of Śiva (sattva, rajas and tamas). You are saffron colored, the Supreme Goddess of the beings of the three worlds, causing the three waves of creation, preservation and destruction. You eternally create and dissolve, fulfilling all desires, raising all beings. Supreme Goddess of the City of Kāśī, be gracious without delay and grant me alms, Supreme Goddess, Mother Annapūrṇā.

- 8 -

देवी सर्वविचित्ररत्नरचिता दक्षकरे संस्थिता
वामस्वादुपयोधरी-सहचरी सौभाग्यमाहेश्वरी ।
भक्ताभीष्टकरी दशाशुभकरी काशीपुराधीश्वरी
भिक्षां देहि कृपावलम्बनकरी माताऽन्नपूर्णेश्वरी ॥

devī sarvavicitraratnaracitā dakṣakare saṁsthitā
vāmasvādupayodharī-sahacarī
saubhāgyamāheśvarī
bhaktābhīṣṭakarī daśāśubhakarī kāśīpurādhīśvarī
bhikṣāṁ dehi kṛpāvalambanakarī
mātā-nnapūrṇeśvarī

Goddess, in your right hand is a golden ladle adorned with various kinds of jewels, and in the left hand is a vessel full of delicious porridge. You are the Supreme Goddess of good fortune, you fulfill the desires of devotees and make destiny propitious. Supreme Goddess of the City of Kāśī, be gracious without delay and grant me alms, Supreme Goddess, Mother Annapūrṇā.

- 9 -

चन्द्रार्कानलकोटिकोटिसदृशा चन्द्रांशुबिम्बाधरी
चन्द्रार्काग्निसमानकुन्तलहरी चन्द्रार्कवर्णेश्वरी ।
मालापुस्तकपाशसांकुशधरी काशीपुराधीश्वरी
भिक्षां देहि कृपावलम्बनकरी माताऽन्नपूर्णेश्वरी ॥

candrārkānalakoṭikoṭisadṛśā candrāṁśubimbādharī candrārkāgnisamānakuntalaharī candrārkavarṇeśvarī mālāpustakapāśasāṁkuśadharī kāśīpurādhīśvarī bhikṣāṁ dehi kṛpāvalambanakarī mātā-nnapūrṇeśvarī

Your radiance is perceived with the illumination of millions of moons, suns and fires. You display a small portion of the moon. Your earrings shine like the moon, sun and fire. You are the Supreme Goddess of the moon, sun and fire. You hold in your hands a mālā, a book, a net and a curved sword. Supreme Goddess of the City of Kāśī, be gracious without delay and grant me alms, Supreme Goddess, Mother Annapūrṇā.

- 10 -

क्षत्रत्राणकरी महाऽभयकरी माता कृपासागरी
साक्षान्मोक्षकरी सदाशिवकरीविश्वेश्वरी श्रीधरी ।
दक्षाक्रन्दकरी निरामयकरी काशीपुराधीश्वरी
भिक्षां देहि कृपावलम्बनकरी माताऽन्नपूर्णेश्वरी ॥

kṣatratrāṇakarī mahā-bhayakarī mātā kṛpāsāgarī sākṣānmokṣakarī sadāśivakarīviśveśvarī śrīdharī dakṣākrandakarī nirāmayakarī kāśīpurādhīśvarī bhikṣāṁ dehi kṛpāvalambanakarī mātā-nnapūrṇeśvarī

You protect the protectors, grant freedom from fear, oh Mother, Ocean of Grace. You are the actual grantor of liberation, the Cause of the eternal Śiva, the Supreme Goddess of the universe, giver of the highest respect. You made Dakṣa lament, you destroy all ills. Supreme Goddess of the City of Kāśī, be gracious without delay and grant me alms, Supreme Goddess, Mother Annapūrṇā.

- 11 -

अन्नपूर्णे सदा पूर्णे शङ्करप्राणवल्लभे ! ।

ज्ञानवैराग्यसिद्ध्यर्थं भिक्षां देहि च पार्वति ! ॥

annapūrṇe sadā pūrṇe śaṅkaraprāṇavallabhe !
jñānavairāgyasiddhyarthaṁ
bhikṣāṁ dehi ca pārvati

Oh Annapūrṇā, who is always full, complete and perfect, beloved energy of Lord Śiva, for the attainment of perfection in wisdom and renunciation, give me alms, Pārvati.

- 12 -

माता च पार्वती देवी पिता देवो महेश्वरः ।

बान्धवाः शिवभक्ताश्च स्वदेशो भुवनत्रयाम् ॥

mātā ca pārvatī devī pitā devo maheśvaraḥ
bāndhavāḥ śivabhaktāśca svadeśo bhuvanatrayām

My mother is the Goddess Pārvatī, my father is the Supreme Lord Maheśvara. My relatives are the devotees of Lord Śiva, and the three worlds are my motherland.

॥ इति श्रीमच्छङ्कराचार्य-विरचित श्रीअन्नपूर्णास्तोत्रं समाप्तः॥

iti śrīmacchaṅkarācārya-viracita
śrīannapūrṇāstotraṁ samāptaḥ

That is the end of the song about Annapūrṇā written by Śaṅkarācārya.

अन्नपूर्णाष्टोत्तरशतनामस्तोत्रम्

annapūrṇāṣṭottaraśatanāmastotram

अस्य श्री अन्नपूर्णष्टोत्तरशतनामस्तोत्रमहामन्त्रस्य,
ब्रह्मा ऋषिः, अनुष्टुप्छन्दः, श्रीअन्नपूर्णेश्वरी देवता,
स्वधाबीजं, स्वाहाशक्तिः, ॐ कीलकं, मम
सर्वाभीष्टप्रसादसिद्ध्यर्थे जपे विनियोगः ।

asya śrī annapūrṇaṣṭottaraśatanāma-stotramahāmantrasya, brahmāṛṣiḥ, anuṣṭupchandaḥ, śrīannapūrṇeśvarī devatā, svadhābījaṁ, svāhāśaktiḥ, oṁ kīlakaṁ, mama sarvābhīṣṭaprasādasiddhyarthe jape viniyogaḥ

Presenting the song of great mantras of one hundred and eight names of the respected Annapūrṇa, Brahmā is the seer; anuṣṭupa is the meter (32 syllables to the verse); the respected Supreme Goddess, Annapūrṇa, is the deity; svadhā, praise of the ancestors, is the seed; svāhā, union with the Gods, is the energy; oṁ is the pin; for the attainment of the fulfillment of my objective, this recitation is being applied.

- 1 -

ॐ अन्नपूर्णा शिवा देवी भीमा पुष्टिरसस्वती ।
सर्वज्ञा पार्वती दुर्गा शर्वाणी शिववल्लभा ॥

oṁ annapūrṇā śivā devī bhīmā puṣṭirasasvatī
sarvajñā pārvatī durgā śarvāṇī śivavallabhā

1 She who is full, complete and perfect with food and grains
2 She who is the energy of the Consciousness of Infinite Goodness
3 She who is the goddess
4 She who is terribly fearful
5 She who gives nourishment

6 She who is eternal
7 She who knows all
8 She who is the daughter of the mountain
9 She who is the reliever of difficulties
10 She who belongs to all
11 She who is the strength of Śiva

- 2 -

वेदवेद्या महाविद्या विद्यादात्री विशारदा ।
कुमारी त्रिपुरा बाला लक्ष्मीश्श्रीर्भयहारिणी ॥

vedavedyā mahāvidyā vidyādātrī viśāradā
kumārī tripurā bālā lakṣmīśśrīrbhayahāriṇī

12 She who knows all knowledge
13 She who is the great knowledge
14 She who is the grantor of knowledge
15 She who is mature
16 She who is the ever pure one
17 She who dwells in the three cities
18 She who is strength
19 She who is the ultimate goal
20 She who is respect
21 She who takes away all fear

- 3 -

भवानी विष्णुजननी ब्रह्मादिजननीतथा ।
गणेशजननी शक्तिः कुमारजननी शुभा ॥

bhavānī viṣṇujananī brahmādijananītathā
gaṇeśajananī śaktiḥ kumārajananī śubhā

22 She who is manifested existence
23 She who is the mother of Viṣṇu
24 She who is the mother of Brahma and the other gods
25 She who is the mother of Ganeśa
26 She who is energy
27 She who is the mother of Kartikeya
28 She who is pure

- 4 -

भोगप्रदा भगवती भक्ताभीष्टप्रदायिनी ।

भवरोगहरा भव्या शुभ्रा परममङ्गला ॥

bhogapradā bhagavatī bhaktābhīṣṭapradāyinī
bhavarogaharā bhavyā śubhrā paramamaṅgalā

29 She who gives enjoyment
30 She who is the supreme goddess
31 She who gives the desired result to devotees
32 She who takes away all disease from the world
33 She who is the attitude of being
34 She who manifests purity
35 She who is the supreme welfare

- 5 -

भवानी चञ्चला गौरी चारुचन्द्रकलाधरा ।

धिश्मलाक्षी विश्वमाता विश्ववन्द्या विलासिनी ॥

bhavānī cañcalā gaurī cārucandrakalādharā
dhiśmalākṣī viśvamātā viśvavandyā vilāsinī

36 She who is being
37 She who is restless
38 She who is rays of light
39 She who supports the attributes of the dark moon
40 She who has big eyes
41 She who is mother of the universe
42 She who is praised by the universe
43 She who is desired

- 6 -

आर्या कस्थाणनिलाया रुद्राणाकमलसना ।

शुभप्रदा शुभावर्ता वृत्तपीनपयोधरा ॥

āryā kasthāṇanilāyā rudrāṇākamalasanā
śubhapradā śubhāvartā vṛttapīnapayodharā

44 She who is purified by knowledge
45 She who rests in welfare
46 She who takes away the tears
47 She who sits upon a lotus
48 She who grants purity
49 She who distributes purity
50 She who shows swelling breasts overflowing with milk

- 7 -

अम्बा संहारमथनी मृडानी सर्वमङ्गला ।
विष्णुसंसेविता सिद्धा ब्रह्माणी सुरसेविता ॥

ambā saṁhāramathanī mṛḍānī sarvamaṅgalā
viṣṇusaṁsevitā siddhā brahmāṇī surasevitā

51 She who is the mother
52 She who churns the ocean of objects and relationships
53 She who is compassionate
54 She who is all welfare
55 She who is served by Viṣṇu
56 She who has attainment
57 She who is the creative energy
58 She who is served by the gods

- 8 -

परमानन्ददा शान्तिः परमानन्दरूपिणी ।
परमानन्दजननी परानन्दप्रदायिनी ॥

paramānandadā śāntiḥ paramānandarūpiṇī
paramānandajananī parānandapradāyinī

59 She who gives the supreme bliss
60 She who is peace
61 She who is the intrinsic nature of the supreme bliss
62 She who is the mother of the supreme bliss
63 She who is an outsider
64 She who is the giver of bliss

- 9 -

परोपकारनिरता परमाभक्तवत्सला ।

पूर्णचन्द्राभवदना पूर्णचन्द्रनिभांशुका ॥

paropakāraniratā paramābhaktavatsalā
pūrṇacandrābhavadanā pūrṇacandranibhāṁśukā

65 She who is always benefiting others
66 She who is the supreme manifestation
67 She who is a pure devotee
68 She who is radiance of the full moon over existence
69 She who is the pure reflection of the full moon

- 10 -

शुभलक्षणसम्पन्ना सुभानन्दगुणार्णवा ।

शुभसौभाग्यनिलया शुभदा च रतिप्रिया ॥

śubhalakṣaṇasampannā subhānandaguṇārṇavā
śubhasaubhāgyanilayā śubhadā ca ratipriyā

70 She who displays all of the pure characteristics
71 She who contains the ocean of purely blissful qualities
72 She who reposes in purely good fortune
73 She who is the giver of purity
74 She who is the beloved of spring

- 11 -

चण्डिका चण्डमथनी चण्डदर्पनिवारिणी ।

मार्तण्डनयना साध्वी चन्द्रग्निनयना सती ॥

caṇḍikā caṇḍamathanī caṇḍadarpanivāriṇī
mārtaṇḍanayanā sādhvī candragninayanā satī

75 She who tears apart all thought
76 She who destroys passion
77 She who destroys the pride of passion
78 She who is the eyes of the sun
79 She who manifests truth and efficiency
80 She whose two eyes are the moon and fire
81 She who is true existence

- 12 -

पुण्डरीकहरापूर्णा पुण्यदा पुण्यरूपिणी ।
मायातीता श्रेष्टमाया श्रेष्ठधर्मात्मवन्दिता ॥

puṇḍarīkaharāpūrṇā puṇyadā puṇyarūpiṇī
māyātītā śreṣṭamāyā śreṣṭadharmātmavanditā

82 She who is the cause of Viṣṇu
83 She who is full, complete and perfect
84 She who is the giver of merit
85 She who is the intrinsic nature of merit
86 She who is beyond māyā
87 She who is the ultimate illusion
88 She who is the ultimate ideal of perfection
89 She who is the praise of the soul

- 13 -

असृष्टिरसङ्गरहिता सृष्टिहेतु कपर्दिनी ।
वृषारूढा शूलहस्ता स्थितिसंहारकारिणी ॥

asṛṣṭirasaṅgarahitā sṛṣṭihetu kapardinī
vṛṣārūḍhā śūlahastā sthitisaṁhārakāriṇī

90 She who is not created
91 She who brings all together in unity
92 She who motivates the creation
93 She who holds a skull
94 She who sits upon a bull
95 She who holds a spear in her hand
96 She who is the cause of creation and dissolution

- 14 -

मन्दस्मिता स्कन्दमाता शुद्धचित्ता मुनिस्तुता ।
महाभगवती दक्षा दक्षाध्वरविनाशिनी ॥

mandasmitā skandamātā śuddhacittā munistutā
mahābhagavatī dakṣā dakṣādhvaravināśinī

97 She who limits laziness
98 She who is the mother of Kartikeya
99 She who is pure consciousness
100 She who is praised by the wise
101 She who is the great supreme goddess
102 She who has ability
103 She who destroyed the activities performed by Dakṣa

- 15 -

सर्वार्थदात्री सावित्री सदाशिवकुटुम्बिनी ।
नित्यसुन्दरसर्वाङ्गी सच्चिदानन्दलक्षणा ॥

sarvārthadātrī sāvitrī sadāśivakuṭumbinī
nityasundarasarvāṅgī saccidānandalakṣaṇā

104 She who is the creator of all objects
105 She who is the daughter of the light
106 She who is the family of the Pure Consciousness of Infinite Goodness
107 She whose every limb is eternally beautiful
108 She who has the character of pure existence, consciousness and bliss

- 16 -

नाम्नामष्टोत्तरशतमम्बायाः पुण्यकारणम् ।
सर्वसौभाग्यसिद्ध्यर्थं जपनीयं प्रयत्नतः ॥

nāmnāmaṣṭottaraśatamambāyāḥ puṇyakāraṇam
sarvasaubhāgyasiddhartharṁ
japanīyaṁ prayatnataḥ

These are the one hundred and eight names, which are the source of great merit. Whoever will recite these names with sincerity will be blessed with all good fortune.

- 17 -

इदञ्जपाधिकारस्तु प्राणमेव ततस्स्तुतः ।
आवहन्तीतिमन्त्रेण प्रत्येकञ्च यथाक्रमम् ॥

idañjapādhikārastu prāṇameva tatasstutaḥ
āvahantītimantreṇa pratyekañca yathākramam

Whoever will recite with their life force (concentrated mind) the songs of the Goddess, and invite Her with the appropriate mantras according to the proper method,

- 18 -

कर्तव्यं तर्पणं नित्यं पीतमन्त्रेतिमूल्वत् ।
तत्तन्मन्त्रेथिहोमेति कर्तव्यश्वेतिमाल्वत् ॥

kartavyaṁ tarpaṇaṁ nityaṁ pītamantretimūlavat
tattanmantrethihometi kartavyaśvetimālavat

and perform the required offerings to the ancestors and forefathers along with the mantras, and then offer the mantras of the sacred fire ceremony, will fill his or her consciousness with attentive perception.

- 19 -

एतानि दिव्यनामानि श्रुत्वाध्यात्वानिरन्तरम् ।
स्तुत्वा देवीञ्च सततं सर्वान्कामानवाप्नुयात् ॥

etāni divyanāmāni śrutvādhyātvānirantaram
stutvā devīñca satataṁ sarvānkāmānavāpnuyāt

These are the divine names, which are to be eternally listened to, contemplated and meditated upon. Whoever will always sing them will attain the fulfillment of all desires.

इति श्रीब्रह्मोत्तरखण्डे आगमप्रख्यातिशिवरहस्ये

अन्नपूर्णाष्टोत्तरशतनामस्तोत्रम् समाप्तम् ।

iti śrībrahmottarakhaṇḍe āgamaprakhyātiśivarahasye annapūrṇāṣṭottaraśatanāmastotram samāptam

Thus ends the divine last section of the secret of the Śiva Āgama called the song of one hundred eight names of Annapūrṇā.

Books by Shree Maa and Swami Satyananda Saraswati

Annapurna Sahasranam
Before Becoming This
Bhagavad Gita
Chandi Path
Cosmic Puja
Devi Gita
Devi Mandir Songbook
Durga Puja Beginner
Ganesh Puja
Hanuman Puja
Kali Dhyanam
Kali Puja
Lakṣmī Sahasranam
Sahib Sadhu, The White Sadhu
Shiva Puja Beginner
Shiva Puja and Advanced Yajna
Shree Maa Cookbook
Shree Maa: The Guru and the Goddess
Shree Maa: The Life of a Saint
Sundar Kanda
Swami Purana

CDs and Cassettes

Chandi Path
Dark Night Mother
Goddess is Everywhere
Lalita Trishati
Mahamrtyunjaya Mantra
Navarna Mantra
Om Mantra
Sadhu Stories from the Himalayas
Shiva is in My Heart
Shiva Puja Beginner (Instructional)
Shiva Puja & Advanced Yajna
Shree Maa in the Temple of the Heart
Shree Maa on Tour 1998
Songs of Ramprasad
Thousand Names of Kali

Videos

Across the States with Shree Maa & Swamiji
Meaning and Method of Worship
Shree Maa: Meeting a Modern Saint
Visiting India with Shree Maa and Swamiji

Please visit us at www.shreemaa.org
Our email is info@shreemaa.org

www.ingramcontent.com/pod-product-compliance
Lightning Source LLC
Chambersburg PA
CBHW021101080526
44587CB00010B/327
* 9 7 8 1 8 7 7 7 9 5 0 8 4 *